I0483833

# SOME CALL IT JUSTICE

By

## MAURO CAPOBIANCO

# SOME CALL IT JUSTICE

## Copyright 2015 by Mauro Capobianco

Published in the United States 2015
ISBN 978-1508434184

# PROLOGUE

It was sixteen minutes past five in the evening when we entered the building. The rookie I had been assigned looked around nervously while I casually moved my nightstick from my right hand to my left. After glancing quickly around the lobby, I started walking toward the door to one of the rear staircases. To a casual observer, I probably appeared quite relaxed, however, my right hand never strayed more than an inch or two from the 38 in my holster. The rookie and I had just entered the lobby of 360 Dumont Avenue, where less than a week ago two cops had been shot when they attempted to arrest two drug dealers.

# Chapter 1

I BEGAN SCANNING THE NEARBY roof tops, looking for anything out of the ordinary. All of a sudden, I could have sworn that I had seen somebody moving on one of the distant roofs. Was it just my imagination? I couldn't really be sure, as it happened so quickly. Thinking that maybe my eyes were playing tricks on me, what with the way the shadows were falling as the sun was setting, I forced myself to look away for a second or two before looking back.

It must have been my imagination after all, as there was nothing to be seen. I was about to turn away thinking that maybe the rookie was right, and it was time to get back down to the street when there was that movement again! This was no figment of my imagination. This time I was positive that there was someone on that roof. It was one of the fourteen-story buildings, over in "Van Dyke Houses". It had to be well over one hundred and fifty yards from here to the other building, making it hard to tell if it was a man or a woman. Adding to the problem was the fact that the roof was encircled by a low brick parapet.

1

Realizing that if I could see whoever it was on that roof, he or she could probably also see me. I quickly crouched down and at the same time hollered over to O'Brien, who had wandered off a short distance to the other end of the roof. Having gotten his attention, I motioned for him to duck down while I pointed in the direction of the other building, hoping that whoever was over there hadn't seen either of us. In no time at all, O'Brien made his way over to where I was crouched. The sullenness of only a few minutes earlier was now replaced with a sense of excitement, which continued to mount as I pointed to the roof where someone could still be seen moving back and forth, behind the low brick parapet. By quickly counting rooftops I figured that it had to be the fourteen-story high-riser on the corner of Blake and Powell.

"Who the hell is it" whispered O'Brien. As if the person on the other roof might be able to hear him.

"Your guess is as good as mine. It's probably some asshole who gets his kicks looking into other people's windows," I said.

"Are we gonna check it out, or are we gonna call it in to Central so they can give the job to the cop who's got the post?" he asked.

"No, we're not calling anything in. I know the cop who has that post, and he's probably four blocks away over on Pitkin Avenue having a couple of slices of pizza" I said. "Besides, he's also known for not answering his radio. Even if he decides to answer the call, by the time he gets his ass over there, whoever the hell is up there now will be long gone."

"So we're going to check it out ourselves?" asked the rookie.

"You catch on pretty quickly, don't you?" I replied, realizing too late how sarcastic I probably sounded and almost regretting it.

The thought of the guy on the other roof had me thinking it could be something. We won't know what, until we get there. Who knows, maybe we might get lucky and catch an early collar.

# Chapter 2

WE HAD BEEN ASSIGNED the Tilden Houses, one of the most dangerous projects in the area of Brooklyn, known as Brownsville. It was October 1979 and with the murder rate well over 2000 homicides a year, you could say that these were dangerous times.

Having begun our four to midnight tour on Rockaway and Dumont, 360 Dumont would be the fourth building on our post. The other four buildings that make up the entire patrol area were one block over on Livonia Avenue facing the El, part of the subway system that runs above ground.

The Rockaway and Livonia station was a favorite of the local purse snatchers. These juveniles, who lived in the projects, would prowl the train station looking for targets. That fact also made it a hunting ground for the undercover cops who worked the neighborhood.

Just as the train doors were about to close, these kids would yank a woman's pocketbook from her and jump through the train's closing doors back onto the platform.

With the pocketbook in hand, they would run down the station stairs to the sidewalk below and disappear into the projects.

In response to pressure from civic groups, plainclothes officers would work the area using unmarked vehicles; they would park near the train's exits where ideally, they could grab the thieves as they hit the sidewalk clutching the stolen pocketbook under their shirts or jackets.

Often, the biggest problem was making contact with the victims, as they were usually still on the train. Thinking that it wouldn't do any good, some of them didn't even bother to report the theft to the police.

Most of the culprits were younger teenagers, so the arrests usually ended up in Children's Court. More often than not, because of the speed with which the crimes occurred, the victims were usually unable to identify the culprits.

Consequently, the arresting officer would be lucky to end up with a final charge of merely possession of stolen property.

These kids knew that, so there was very little deterrence to stopping them from committing these types of crimes.

However, once they reached their 16th birthday, they were prosecuted in Criminal Court. They were still classified as adolescents, but there was at least the possibility of them getting some jail time.

It had taken the rookie and me a little over an hour to check the first three buildings, which basically involved searching the stairwells and hallways for anyone intent on committing a crime.

Once in a while, you would get lucky and come across a kid rifling through a pocketbook or a stolen wallet. They would be mostly kids, who after snatching the purse, had managed to elude the cops near the train station.

Then there were the junkies, like heroin addicts, they would duck into the buildings to "shoot up" drugs that they had just bought out on the street.

In addition to settling a heated argument in front of the entrance of one of the buildings between a mother and her teenaged daughter; we had scared off a group of older black males who were engaged in a crap game, in the rear of the lobby of 320 Dumont. Engrossed with the game, they hadn't seen us walking into the building until it was almost too late!

One of the players just happened to look our way as we entered the lobby and shouted "Police!" with that, they all jumped up and ran out the back door of the building.

They left behind a small pile of dollar bills, along with the dice on the floor of the lobby, and rather than trying to chase them, I nonchalantly bent over and gathered up the money, noting that it totaled $16.00. The rookie looked at me and said, "What are you gonna do with the money?"

I said, "You know, I don't know, I guess I'll turn it in to the Widows and Orphans Fund at the end of the tour".

More likely, it would pay for the pizza I was already planning for our meal later in the evening. Of course I didn't tell him that. Often, the less a rookie knew, the better off he was.

While things thus far had been pretty quiet for a Friday evening, that could all change in the blink of an eye. You never knew if turning the next corner would bring you face to face with a madman, wildly swinging a machete at someone, or a teenager waving a gun at rival gang members. He could be on the verge of shooting them, when all of a sudden you'll turn the corner and you are now face to face and it's suddenly show time!

In the blink of an eye, the rival gang members are no longer of any concern to him. You've now become his number one problem. Shooting you instead of them has just become a real possibility. Hopefully, he drops the gun, and a tragedy is averted. Often times, however, a shoot-out occurs, and someone is either wounded or killed! What could happen from one minute to the next is anyone's guess.


I remember one incident in particular. It was in the early hours of the morning around 4:00 a.m. Up until then, it had been a pretty uneventful Monday morning during a 12 to 8 tour.

My partner and I had been minding our own business, quietly cruising up and down the deserted neighborhood streets with our lights off, when all of a sudden we pull up on a shooting in progress in front of one of the old abandoned tenements on Stone Avenue. The guy doing the shooting was a black male who looked to be in his late sixties. He was shooting at another black male, who looked to be about the same age. The poor guy who was being shot at was holding up an empty aluminum garbage can between him and the shooter, valiantly trying to ward off the bullets. The garbage can had been sitting at the curb for who knows how long, and it was the only thing that the victim could think of to get behind. Luckily for him, the shooter was so drunk that he didn't realize that he could have just as easily shot straight through the thin metal can, which the intended victim was using as a sort of shield while screaming. The shooter, apparently quite drunk, was bobbing and weaving, trying to shoot around the can as the victim kept moving in circles trying to keep from getting shot. Miraculously, he wasn't even wounded!

Seeing the scene unfold, I quickly hit the brakes, and both my partner and I jumped from the vehicle, shouting "Freeze, police, drop the gun!"

Fortunately, the shooter, not hearing us drive up was taken by surprise and upon hearing the word police, turned in our direction. He immediately dropped the gun to the ground, and raised both his hands in the air. Had he not complied as quickly as he did, we would have been forced to shoot him. I know that if I had fired my weapon, I probably would have not only shot him, but also his intended victim.

As the shooter turned with his hands in the air, the victim lowered the garbage can and began shouting, "Officer, officer your car, your car!"

It was only then, that I remembered that I hadn't taken the patrol car out of drive, and the car was now slowly rolling down the street. Lou, my partner, saw the car, took off running, and caught up with it before it had hit anything.

He was able to easily jump back in the car, because I hadn't closed the door. Believe it or not, things like that do happen, although not that often thank God!

My heart rate returned to normal as Lou drove the car to where I was standing with the prisoner. The victim, probably due to a case of nerves, couldn't stop laughing. Meanwhile the shooter kept mumbling in his drunken state, "I's so sorry, I's so sorry."

I guess you could say that everyone was a winner. We were able to prevent a possible homicide. We made a felony arrest and recovered a gun in the process. Both Lou and I, about a year later, received a Medal of Exceptional Merit award. Thankfully, the prisoner, the victim, and certainly neither of us ever mentioned the runaway patrol car.

As the saying goes, further investigation disclosed that the two men were actually the best of friends. The whole event was one big misunderstanding!

The shooter, Willie, had picked up his buddy Carl from the Port Authority Bus terminal in Manhattan on Friday evening. Carl had travelled up from Charlotte, North Carolina, and was going to spend a week in the Big Apple partying with Willie. They had both started drinking, not too long after Carl got off the bus. When 4:00 AM Monday morning rolled around, and just before we arrived on the scene, Carl made the big mistake of finishing off the last of the pint of Orange Rock that they had been amicably sharing. That was perceived as inconsiderate on his part and that set off the altercation. All hell broke loose when Willie went to help himself to a taste and found the bottle completely empty. That was when Willie's gun came out and the shooting began.

These types of occurrences are fairly common in Brownsville. If you hoped to make it to retirement in one piece, you had better learn early in your career the ways of the streets. Rule number one, always, and I mean always, expect the unexpected. The cops that didn't develop that mentality early on in their careers were doomed to one of two things. An ulcer from the constant worry and stress of the job, or worse yet, getting killed in the line of duty and becoming the recipient of an Inspector's Funeral!

With a little luck, you could avoid falling victim to both of those outcomes, and retire to sunny Florida.

# Chapter 3

MY NAME IS MARTINO CAPORUSSO, and I've been a housing cop in Brooklyn for a little over fifteen years. For the past ten of those fifteen years, I was a detective.

I'd racked up a number of good arrests, making the Daily News on several occasions, and that got me an interview for a detective's gold shield, fairly early in my career. Up until a few weeks ago, other than some minor ups and downs, I really had very little to bitch about. Then, without any warning, the proverbial shit hit the fan!

I am no longer a detective; and I am now pretty much back to square one. I am once again, a patrolman. You're probably saying to yourself, he must have done something really bad. I mean detectives get demoted for serious things, don't they?

Well, for lack of a better explanation, my hook, rabbi, benefactor or whatever else you might want to call him, had been forced to retire. I and quite a few others who were associated with him got caught up in the purge. For him, it was either retire or be reduced to the rank of captain.

What you need to understand is that while I technically did work out of headquarters in Manhattan, I spent all of my time in Brooklyn. While Inspector Campbell was the person that I reported to, you couldn't say that he and I were close enough to be on a first name basis. I called him "Sir" and he called me Cappy, unless he was angry, and then I'd rather not repeat what he called me! As far as his demotion to captain, from what I was able to determine, had he decided to challenge it and not won, he would have stood to lose a pretty large sum of money from his pension.

While it was rumored that he had made some enemies on his rise up through the ranks, he had never really hurt anyone. Nor could anyone accuse him of any serious wrongdoing. His enemies for the most part were individuals who felt that they, and not him deserved the promotions and advancements to command positions.

His attitude with those of us who served him had always been that so long as you did your job, you had nothing to worry about. Of course I'm partial. He was my boss and he was good to not only me but also to the other detectives who worked for him.

The bottom line was that someone wanted him out, and their man in, and it was going to happen regardless of who was hurt in the process. I am convinced that whoever orchestrated the Inspector's removal was definitely from City Hall. Exactly who that person was, we'll probably never know. Whoever it was had the mayor's ear. In fact, the scuttlebutt making its way around headquarters was that the Inspector and the Deputy Chief had been informed of their demotions that morning at an 8 o'clock meeting with the Chief.

The Deputy Chief, Bob Lefee, was fortunate to have a few friends himself who were influential enough to slow the process and were able to get them both a small reprieve. The new Chief was forced to back down, and they were both given until noon to submit their retirement papers, thereby avoiding their demotions to captain in addition to the corresponding loss of thousands of dollars from their pensions.

I was truly shocked when I heard of his being pushed out the door. When something like that happens to one of the higher ups, the word spreads through the job like wildfire. I had spent the entire morning trying to reach him by phone, hoping that he would be able to tell me that it was all bullshit, and that he wasn't going anywhere, and even more importantly to me, that my job was safe. While I felt bad for him, all I could think about was how this change would affect me personally, and more specifically, my assignment to special investigations.

I had this feeling of impending doom. I knew that it was only a matter of when and not if I would lose my detective shield, and be returned to uniform patrol. With less than five years to go before I could retire, there was no way in hell that I could ever earn back the gold shield. I knew that I had to resign myself to the fact that I would have to get used to the idea that I would retire as "Patrolman Caporusso", and not detective.

"As per General Order No.746/81, Det.3rd Grade Martino Caporusso, Shield 2746, is hereby demoted to police officer and is ordered to report to headquarters for the issuance of a new ID card, and patrolman's shield" was how the teletype had spelled it out.

Apparently, the powers that be weren't content with just pushing the Inspector, and the Deputy Chief out the door. They had to wreak havoc with the people who had personally worked for him, namely yours truly, and about ten other good cops working special assignments.

There was a captain, who used to show deference to me because of how closely I worked with the Inspector. When he saw me for the first time, several days after Inspector Campbell's departure, he made it a point to sneer "You know when you live by the sword, you die by the sword", implying that the Inspector got what he had coming to him. This is the same captain who used to frequently remind me to "give the Inspector my regards when you see him."

# Chapter 4

I **QUICKLY GLANCED AROUND** the lobby. With the exception of a few people waiting for the elevators to arrive, nothing appeared suspicious or out of the ordinary. I had checked the time as we were approaching the front of the building, making a note of it and now took a moment to record that information in my memo book.

My partner for the next eight hours, Probationary Patrolman William O'Brien, looked over my shoulder as I was entering the information. He had, as per my instructions, written an identical entry in his memo book.

He then smiled and in an exaggerated Irish brogue said. "So, Officer Martino, now what are we supposed to do?"

He knew full well that calling me by my given name, Martino would piss me off, and he seemed to not give a shit! I began to suspect that I was going to have a bit of a problem with this kid.

At roll call, I had specifically told him that he should call me Cappy, and never mind the Martino, which is how that donkey lieutenant had introduced me. I know that I'm sounding a bit unreasonable, but I never could quite wrap my head around the name I had been given at birth.

Maybe I should take a moment and explain the name Martino, a name that resulted in me being picked on constantly by the nuns all through elementary school (most of whom were Irish), and continued by the brothers(again mostly Irish) through High School.

I'd discovered years ago at one of our family reunions that it had been my grandmother who had come up with the idea of naming me Martino. It had been explained to me by one of my uncles that it had to do with her fascination with a famous wrestler by the name of Bruno San Martino.

God bless my grandmother Maria. She didn't speak a word of English, having been born in Italy and immigrated to America at the age of sixteen. My grandfather Giuseppe, who had been born in Brooklyn, lived next door to the newly arrived immigrant family. He took one look at their daughter Maria and knew he would take her as his bride. He eventually convinced her father to allow him to marry the young Maria. Now, my grandfather, who also had immigrant parents, had a total of twenty-five brothers and sisters. You have to remember that there was no TV back then. My grandfather being old-fashioned believed, as did his father that a happy marriage meant keeping your wife barefoot in the winter and pregnant in the summer, and he did just that. My grandmother fell short of her husband's family of twenty-six, but still managed to give birth to four sons and three daughters.

From what I've been told, what seemed to slow my grandfather down from having an even larger family was my grandmother's fascination with television. He made the mistake of buying one of the first sets to hit the market. That was the beginning of her fascination with wrestling, and in particular, her hero, "Bruno San Martino." who was obviously "Italian!"

She also took care of both me and my cousin Joe for a couple of years while both our moms worked in defense plants during the Second World War. Although I spent my toddler years with my grandmother Maria; as a teenager I never really got to know her. She passed away from cancer in 1954 at the age of 56.

At the time I was living at a military boarding school in Pennsylvania. My Dad, not wanting to leave my mother's side while she grieved sent my uncle Vinnie out to pick me up and drive me back to New York for the funeral.

I was twelve at the time and had never been to a funeral. Back then, they didn't use a professional funeral home.

Consequently, her open coffin sat in the living room for three days while friends and relatives came by to pay their respects.

I'll never forget how cold her face felt on my lips when I kissed her cheek before they closed the coffin for the trip to the church. That coldness stayed with me for several weeks back at school.

My aunt Virginia, my mother's youngest sister, sort of inherited my grandmother's old six-inch screen black and white TV after my grandfather passed away.

It was eventually passed on to me after my discharge from the army in 1962. I had settled on Long Island, not too far from where Aunt Virginia lived. I was renting a room in the upstairs portion of a private home in Huntington Station. Oddly, that TV became as much a companion to me as it had been to my grandmother Maria.

At the time, Johnny Carson, a newcomer to late night TV, helped get me through many nights in that small rented room.

As much as I loved my grandmother, I didn't like being called "Martino". Fortunately, while I was still in the academy, my classmates started calling me Cappy and the nickname has stuck with me ever since.

# Chapter 5

**HAVING COMPLETED MY MEMO** book entry, I checked O'Brien's book to make sure he hadn't made any errors. In my former position of detective, I didn't nor was I really expected to maintain a memo book on a daily basis, which was just fine with me. The book was more than just a record of events that happened during a tour of duty. It was also a supervisory tool. A sergeant was required to inspect an officer's book at least once in an eight-hour period. He would scrawl his name plus the date and time in the officer's book. This made it impossible for officers to back date information about incidents that may have occurred during their tours. Your book better be current when the boss drove up and asked to see it.

Conversely, as a detective, no one really expected you to bother with a memo book. We were above all that, what with reports and statements that we took from both the victims and the perps. My personal philosophy had always been the less you put in writing, the safer you were. Sure, it didn't fit in with the department's philosophy, then again, not fitting in was a problem that I've had for a very long time.

14

Having been put back in uniform meant that I like everyone else, had to toe the line and that definitely included the bullshit with the books. There were a number of Irish bosses who would like nothing better than to get at an "eye-talian," especially this one.

Being back on foot patrol provided those bosses a wide assortment of minor infractions that they could conjure up if necessary.

Until recently, I was untouchable. That I had been assigned this rookie from the academy only made it more imperative that for the next eight hours I walk a straight line. I didn't like working with rookies, and I was even more uncomfortable working with this one after I had heard that he had an uncle who was a sergeant assigned to the Internal Affairs Bureau! As the saying goes, "Just because you're paranoid, doesn't mean that they're not out to get you!"

I seriously considered asking him if it were true that he had an uncle in IAB. However, after giving it some further thought, I decided not to. It could open up a whole can of worms that I'd rather not explore.

You had to be very careful when dealing with cops of Irish descent. I don't want to sound prejudiced, but there was a time when the Irish ran the police department. I've heard the stories about how the Italians were routinely referred to as dagos and guineas, or even wops, and how at roll call they were routinely told, "You dagos line up in the back row." Of course these ethnic slurs occurred back in the early nineteenth century. A lot has changed since then. However, some of the old timers who were exposed to this bigotry while growing up eventually became bosses and they still harbor feelings of ill will towards us wops.

The desk lieutenant finally called the 28 officers to attention, and we formed into three rows all facing toward. At about the same time, one of the Patrol Sergeants brought in about seven rookies and an audible groan emanated from the assembled group. The sergeant directed the rookies to fall in behind everyone else, making up a fourth row.

This was a Friday night ritual whenever a class was being processed through the academy. These officers, like their fellow recruits throughout the city, would be assigned to various housing projects and paired with experienced officers for the four to midnight tours.

The lieutenant began reading the assignments, stopping occasionally to pair a rookie to a particular officer. I breathed a silent sigh of relief in that he had disposed of all of the rookies before he had reached me.

I had been spared! I have nothing against training new officers. What annoys me is their habit of going back to the academy on Monday morning and exaggerating everything that had taken place during their tour of field training. Not wanting to be outdone by their classmates, some of them told stories bordering on the bizarre, and that could sometimes result in a problem for the training officer the rookie had been paired with.

Fortunately this was not to be one of my concerns, as I was assigned to a foot post in the area of Tilden Houses, which meant that I could look forward to an early collar. Little did I know what was to come.

# Chapter 6

**WELL HERE WE ARE** and yours truly is still on the job, although now in newly purchased uniforms. The old ones that I hadn't worn in over ten years no longer fit. All fourteen of us that had worked exclusively for the Inspector were returned to uniform patrol. The new chief insisted that the demotions were in no way connected to Inspector Campbell's retirement, but were due to budgetary constraints. Of course, no one really believed that, but none of us dared complain because of what he had been able to do to our boss.

It was a quarter to four in the afternoon, and I was in Police Service Area #2, which is basically the station house for the Housing PD (Police Department) in the east end of Brooklyn. In the old days we reported for duty to what were known as Record Rooms. Now, with centralization, we have PSAs throughout the city. I was standing in the area of the Desk, that long high elevated counter that exists in almost every police station in the nation. Standing behind the Desk usually can be found either a sergeant or lieutenant, who routinely conducts roll calls at the beginning of each tour.

I had changed into my uniform and was now standing off by myself, waiting for roll call to begin. While I knew most of the fifteen or so other cops, none of them had anything to say to me. I like to believe that they were too embarrassed for me and why I was there in uniform.

I began to wonder just where I might be assigned today. Since returning to uniform, I had been drawing some real lousy foot posts. I was convinced that it wasn't accidental. However, once out there it usually took me no more than an hour to come up with some sort of an arrest.

This meant that I had to be picked up and transported back to the PSA with the prisoner. Once the paperwork was completed, the prisoner and I were then transported down to Central Booking.

This pissed off certain supervisors. These bosses were bent on seeing me spend the whole eight hours alone, walking a foot post in some of the most dangerous areas of Brownsville.

My reaction to this kind of harassment was to arrest the first junkie I caught carrying drugs. Granted, it may have been a bullshit collar, but there wasn't a thing they could do about it. Unlike the City PD, who were required to call a sergeant to the scene of an arrest so he could give it his blessing, Housing Cops just made the collar, and the sergeant found out about it later, if at all.

Sergeant O'Leary has been on the job for the past thirty years. He should have retired ten years ago, after failing the lieutenant's exam four times, but being the hard-headed donkey that he is, he stayed on. Now one of his goals is to break my balls as often as he can.

He had realized right after roll call that I hadn't been assigned a rookie. He couldn't let that happen. He made it his business to alter the roll call, and bingo, I was assigned a rookie. Not just any rookie, but one named William O'Brien. The young looking kid had four months of academy training behind him, and with only one more month to go, it wasn't like this was his first time out on the street. He looked to be no more than twenty-two or twenty-three and was a little on the heavy side, probably 190 or so. At 5'10, that kind of weight put him in the heavy category. He could probably take care of himself. Regardless of all those fine young attributes, he was still a rookie. If you polled any number of veteran cops, you'd find very few who didn't have a problem working with these kids. We all knew that they had to gain experience by being with a trained officer before being sent out on their own, but none of the cops that I knew wanted to be the ones guiding them.

There were certainly a lot of cops named O'Brien in the Department, and I think that the IAB rumor was started just to stress me out, especially since the rookie was O'Leary's idea! I was also worried that being the prick that he was, he might suggest to one of the other supervisors that perhaps Cappy could do with a little "closer supervision."

# Chapter 7

**ALL OF THESE CONCERNS BROUGHT** back the memory of how good I'd had it. My career was indeed on the fast track that is until I found myself back in the bag. My previous assignment, again thanks to the Inspector, had been with the Economic Crimes Unit of the Brooklyn DA's office. I was working on Arson for Profit Investigations, which was the result of my making an arrest for the attempted arson of a local business. I interrupted two Spanish speaking males who at three in the morning were bent on pouring two gallons of gasoline in and around a bodega in Brownsville.

For several years preceding that assignment with the DA's office, I'd been doing special investigations out of Inspector Campbell's office, who was in charge of the entire Patrol Bureau.

Unfortunately, all good things must come to an end. I just never in a million years thought that it would apply to me. I guess I should be thankful that I still have a job. I read the teletype several times before I was convinced that it was on the level and not someone's idea of a cruel joke, thought up by the likes of O'Leary.

I had never personally done anything to Sergeant O'Leary, but I guess my comments over the years about his beloved "Emerald Society," must not have sat too well with him. With him on the desk, I wasn't taking any chances. Tonight the rules and procedures were going to be followed.

Learning how to cover your butt early on was sometimes more important than learning how to shoot straight. This covering your butt mindset was especially true when it came to dealing with the rookies. They had their own creative way of embellishing things and exaggerating what had happened while out on their Friday night training tours. Creative ways that would put a veteran used car salesman to shame. More than one cop had found that out the hard way!

It had to have been a couple of months ago, during the heat wave in August, when a cop named Jordan was working with one of the rookies. They had taken their meal in the rear storeroom of one of the local bodegas. The place was on their post, so they were legit. That they hadn't illegally gone off post, a big violation of the R & Ps, which turned out was the least of their problems.

While the two officers were eating their sandwiches, the veteran officer made the mistake of accepting a cold beer from the store owner. The officer then made the even bigger mistake of allowing the rookie to do the same.

The incident took place during the rookie's Friday night field duty. The following Monday morning back at the academy, the rookie couldn't stop bragging to his buddies about how he and his training officer had eaten "on the arm," and washed down their sandwiches with a couple of free beers to boot. He went on to say that he hadn't realized that there were so many perks to being a cop.

It wasn't long before the brass down at the academy got wind of the incident, and Internal Affairs was called in to investigate.

The rookie had been spared, which is usually the way it goes down. Had it been behavior that rose to the level of a felony, I mean two really expensive sandwiches; well then the rookie also would have been toast.

The cop, Jordan, had taken all the so-called weight, and that little peccadillo had cost him ten days of vacation time. Internal Affairs had recommended termination. Fortunately for Jordan, he had several commendations for a couple of good collars, so IAB was forced to back down. The only positive thing to come out of the whole incident was that Patrolman Jordan was prohibited from being paired with a rookie. The rumor circulating around the station house was that Jordan was really torn up over that decision, if you know what I mean. Just to show how badly it had affected him, he took about a week's worth of paid sick time to overcome it.

# Chapter 8

**I'D HAD MORE THAN MY FAIR SHARE** of problems lately and I wasn't looking to add any new ones to the list. I wasn't about to give a patrol supervisor the chance to hit me with a complaint like, "improper patrol."

The lobby of the sixteen story building wasn't crowed at this time of the evening. A few hours from now would be another story. Most of the "working stiffs" were not yet on their way home from work, not that there were that many in this neighborhood to begin with. The other members of the community, who didn't find the concept of work that appealing, were out hustling up some money to party with later.

After we paused a few minutes to get our books caught up. We began checking both the first and second floor staircases, which turned up clean. Sometimes, if you got lucky you'd come upon a couple of teenagers hanging around in the stairwells, watching and waiting for a chance to rob some unsuspecting little old lady. This usually was a lady who made the mistake of venturing out to do some shopping at a local store. These predators would wait and watch from the stairwell until the elderly person had inserted their key into the apartment's locked door. Once the door was open, they would run up behind the victim and push them the rest of the way into the apartment. Once inside they would grab whatever was handy, and use it to tie the senior citizen to a chair. They would then begin searching the apartment to see what they could steal. During one such robbery, not finding anything of value they got angry and set the apartment on fire, killing the person who was bound to the chair. The fire destroyed most of the apartment before the fire department was able to put it out. The scumbags were ultimately apprehended and they turned out to be two young boys, both twelve years of age.

Having found both stairwells empty we went back to the lobby. Once back in the lobby, I pressed the button for the elevator. We took the elevator to the top floor and checked the roof landings, the area at the top of the last flight of stairs leading to the roof's door. I had no problem walking up a couple of flights of stairs; however, five was my limit. At my age, and what with the shape that I was in, there was no way that I could even think of negotiating sixteen flights.

As a form of entertainment some of the more inventive teenagers would somehow disable the two elevators and then call 911 to report "a man with a gun on the sixteenth floor."

Coming over the radio as a gun run energized everyone on patrol, so you might get eight to ten cops responding. The teenagers who called 911, who were waiting on the 16th floor, got a kick out of seeing how the cops looked after climbing all those stairs.

The more experienced housing cops would pause in the stairwell on the 15th floor, catch their breath and then climb the last flight ready to do battle without being winded. Of course once on the 16th floor there would be no man with a gun to be found. The more aggressive officers would start kicking the shit out of anyone who thought the whole episode was funny. Usually, a couple of loiterers would get a free ride to central booking, with a brief stop at the hospital's emergency room!

In short order one of the elevators arrived, and we got on. Once inside I pressed the button for the 16th floor and we were on our way up. O'Brien must have sensed the fact that I was still a little pissed since the Martino remark, as he hadn't said much since then. When the elevator finally came to a stop, the door slid open and we both stepped out. He paused momentarily waiting for me to tell him which one of the two staircases leading up to the roof that I wanted him to take. They instruct the rookies back at the academy that under no circumstances are they to ever leave the side of the officer they're assigned to and for the most part that's pretty much the way it is.

One exception to that rule is when you check roof landings, since in most of the taller buildings there are usually two staircases leading to the roof. Each officer takes a separate staircase and then they both meet up again on the roof. If once out on the roof you aren't immediately joined by the other officer, you would suspect that something or someone was holding the other cop back. You'd then immediately go to the other roof landing door to back him up. If a perp was on the roof landing and he heard someone enter the staircase below, he would think that it was probably a cop. In all likelihood he'd panic and bolt out the door onto the roof. If everything clicked, the other officer would be in a position to make the apprehension. Had anyone been on the roof landing shooting up drugs, or better yet, rifling through a recently snatched women's pocketbook, he would have been trapped by the approaching officer and unable to escape.

Such was not the case on this fall evening, as both roof landings were empty. I did see some evidence of recent drug use on the landing that I had checked.

Once on the roof and making sure that it was clear, I saw O'Brien standing in a corner over at the other end. Figuring that I had an opportunity to clue him in on a few things, I called him over to where I was standing. As he got closer I told him that I had something to show him. I opened the large metal door that I had just moments before come through. I pointed to a bottle cap on the floor just inside the doorway and asked him,

"What do you see?'

"It looks like the cap to a soda bottle."

"While a bottle cap," I said "may not be all that significant to the average person, the fact that it contains a small balled up piece of cotton in addition to a women's bobby pin attached to it is definitely significant to us."

"Someone was up here, and from the look of things, probably not too long ago. Whoever it was, they sure left in one hell of a hurry"

"What makes you say that?" said O'Brien, "How can you be so sure?"

"Junkies are not known to leave half their set of works behind" I said and continued.

"Whoever it was didn't even wait long enough for the "high" to kick in. That's probably his blood over by the stairs"

Not too far from the bottle cap was the indispensable bottle of water which I pointed out to him, and said,

"The bottle has water in it, a junkie only needs just enough to cook the heroin. They pour a little water into the bottle cap, add the powdered heroin, and hold a lit match under the cap. They hold onto the bottle cap with the attached bobby pin to keep from burning their fingers."

Feeling as if I were on a roll, I continued,

"In no time at all the heroin mixes with the heated water. Once that's done the small cotton ball comes into play and acts like a filter through which the heroin is sucked up into an old insulin syringe. A belt becomes a tourniquet and is applied to their upper arm, as soon as a vein pops up; they inject the drug into their arm.   The whole process from start to finish takes about two minutes. When I come across a bottle of water like that I'll dump it out. I figure, not having the water available slows them down a bit. Other cops aren't as nice about it, and have been known to add things to the water hoping that the next junkie to come along will be in too much of a hurry to notice the ....odor.

"You gotta be kidding. Cops would actually do something like that?" he asked.  That shocked look on his face

26

convinced me that I probably should have kept my big mouth shut. I better be more careful about what I say for the rest of the time that he and I are together.

I continued more cautiously, "It isn't very often that you'd catch a junkie on a roof landing. I'd say a good guess would be that this guy was up here sometime between three and four this afternoon. They knew when the cops changed shifts, and that the chances that one might surprise them shooting up during those times was very slim. Once in a while you might come across one who had gotten a load of some extra strong heroin and just nodded off with the needle still stuck in his arm."

"Would they be dead at that point?' he asked.

"No, but they'd be pretty close." I said. "They were the ones you'd find who were oblivious to what was happening around them. They would be just lying on the roof landing, unconscious. I dreaded those times the most. They then became what we referred to as "aided cases", I'm sure they told you about them at the academy."

"We touched on it briefly, not as much as we did with the cardiac cases." He said.

"Well on these junkie cases", I continued, "an ambulance has to be summoned, and in most instances, you'd have to accompany the individual to the hospital. Now don't get me wrong, there are cops who look forward to the ride to the hospital which gets them off the street for a couple of hours. Personally, I prefer to spend my time looking for collars and not sitting in the emergency room."

The kid looked at me as if I'd just grown horns.

"Isn't it just as much our job to help people like that, as much as it is to make arrests?" he said.

"Listen kid, I'm not saying that you shouldn't help people, drug addicts or not. All I'm saying is that given a choice, I would rather spend my time fighting crime and not babysitting someone in a hospital. Maybe in my next life I'll become a male nurse, who knows?"

"It should be noted" he says, "that in New York, being a heroin addict is not a criminal offense."

SOME CALL IT JUSTICE

"Yes, you're right. I said, "Which is one of the reasons why we have so many addicts. Listen, I really don't want to debate the issue with you. Apparently we have a difference of opinion when it comes to addicts. You keep your opinion and I'll keep mine. OK?"

Again, I should have kept my big mouth shut. Here I am trying to clue him in on some of the things that I picked up over the years, and he wants to have a debate.

"Getting back to the unconscious junkie" I say. "Sometimes, you didn't have a choice in the matter, since you couldn't just step over an unconscious body and walk away. Well, let's just say you weren't supposed to walk away. However, discovering a junkie on a roof landing didn't occur that often as they were usually one step ahead of the police.

"Can I keep the bottle cap?" asked O'Brien. "I'd like to take it to class on Monday to show the other guys."

"What's that like a sort of show and tell" I said jokingly.

"Well, it would certainly beat anything the other guys have brought back from Field Training. It would also score me some points with the instructors, as it would show that I was actually out doing the job." said O'Brien in a more serious tone of voice.

I guess he didn't appreciate my little attempt at humor with the "show and tell" comment.

After placing the bottle cap in his pocket, he turned to me, and in that same serious voice said,

"Shouldn't we be getting back down to the street? Maybe we could check another building, before it gets any later"

Sensing the obvious sarcasm in his voice, which wasn't the least bit lost on me. I decided, then and there that he needed some straightening out. I was the senior officer and he was the rookie and I was the one who called the shots, not him!

"Listen kid", I began. "One of the secrets to surviving on this job and hopefully making it to retirement is to take it slow and easy and not be in such a hurry to look for trouble. Trouble will always find you. What you need to do is to develop your ability to look out for trouble, if you know what I mean. I'll tell you a story that goes back many years ago to when I was appointed. We were standing in formation at the academy on the day that we were sworn in, when one of the bosses said,

"Take a good look at the guy on your left and the guy on your right". He then went on to say that in the next twenty years, one of them will be dead! At the time most of us thought the guy was just trying to impress us. Well, over the next fifteen years, I attended both their funerals; the one on my left was killed just before his 13th year, and the one on my right, a year later."

With that said, I seemed to have gotten his attention, so I continued.

"As you can see I'm still here, so I must be doing something right. Now think about it, here we are up here on a roof sixteen stories above the street with no apparent danger lurking about. So try to relax a bit and enjoy the view. We'll go back down when I say so, and not a minute sooner. Have I made myself clear?"

"Yes sir." He replied.

"Do you have any questions?"

"No Sir' he said and mumbled something under his breath as he slowly turned and ambled off towards the other end of the roof. I walked the short distance toward the wrought iron railing that encircled the perimeter of the roof. From this height you could easily see over the roof tops of the many nearby smaller buildings of the older "Brownsville Houses". It never ceased to amaze me, looking down at the street and sidewalks below how a neighborhood like this with all its' crime and violence could seem so peaceful from up here almost 200 feet above the sidewalk. Except for the wailing sirens of the fire department's vehicles, that always seemed to be on the move, the streets below looked anything but threatening. The landscape appeared even more serene than usual owing perhaps to the scarcity of pedestrians walking about due to the autumn chill in air as the sun was about to set in the western sky.

# Chapter 9

**MAYBE IT WAS THE THOUGHT** of the western sky that all of a sudden had me remembering an experience that I'd had as a kid, many years ago.

There was this hill back in the early 50s, not too far from where we lived in Brooklyn. I'm pretty sure it was made up of an ever increasing mound of garbage although being a kid; I didn't think that at the time. We lived near the hill, but not close enough to where you could smell the garbage. Our house as I recall was on East 73rd Street which was a dead end street off of Avenue U. I could see the hill from our front stoop.

Thinking back all those years, it was around this time of day with the sun setting. On that particular afternoon I was sitting on the stoop thinking of nothing in particular. When I looked up and saw six or seven people on horseback, riding on a trail over the top of that hill. They rode in single file and were silhouetted against the sky as the sun was setting. All were heading back to the riding academy that I knew to be over on Ralph Avenue.

One minute I'm gazing at the sunset over the tops of the housing projects and in the next breath I've been transported back twenty-five years in time. While these thoughts are drifting through my head, they're also joined by an old cowboy song sung by a singer with a very deep voice. I can hear the sound of his voice, but I've long since forgotten his name. The song was entitled, Ghost Riders in the Sky, and while most of the words escaped me the tune didn't. What is it that being up here high above the surrounding buildings caused me to drift back all those years? What brought about these memories of twenty-five years ago, especially the old tune that hasn't been around since the early fifties, is beyond me.

A shrink would probably say that I was subconsciously longing to return to a simpler time of my life. That shrink, considering how I had been faring lately, especially with the demotion, would probably be right on the money. The song coupled with the image brought back old memories of growing up in Bergen Beach, a section of Brooklyn that really had no beach! Not unless you counted the polluted water that flowed from the landfill and meandered beneath the Belt Parkway Bridge, emptying into Jamaica Bay.

The neighborhood I'm speaking of is not that far from where I now stood looking over the nearby rooftops. The distance is probably not more than 5 miles, but in reality, the neighborhoods might as well have been worlds apart.

I know that it has been said more than enough times, but I'm going to say it once again, anyway. There was definitely a lot less crime back in the old days. The thought that someone would enter your home while you were not there, and walk away with everything that you owned, was just unimaginable.

Contrary to what the social scientists would have you believe, the fifties was a really great time to be growing up in America, at least that's how I remember it. Then again, I didn't become a cop until the mid-sixties, so until then, what did I know about crime?

The current talk from the so called liberals, who never seem to get tired of repeating themselves, is that the fifties was one of the most repressive periods in our history. They are quick to resurrect the likes of some guy named Joe McCarthy, and his commie witch hunts, as examples.

I remember my Dad being engrossed in the Senate Sub Committee hearings on TV and watching someone speaking before a bank of microphones. Other than that, I knew nothing, nor did I care about, Communists.

My opinion remains unchanged and still is that the streets were a lot safer then and people were also nicer than they are today.

Thinking of crime brought me back to the present and the projects the rookie and I are supposed to be patrolling. Just as suddenly as the ghost rider's apparition had appeared, it just as suddenly disappeared.

# Chapter 10

**HOPEFULLY, MY LUCK WAS CHANGING.** At the very least the rookie and I have a collar for criminal trespass. Everyone who lives in the projects knows that the roofs are strictly off limits and if he's not a tenant, with a little creative writing I can maybe work it up to a Burglary.

If we move fast enough we can get up there before whoever he is, decides to leave. In any event it will give the rookie a chance to work off some of that nervous energy. Besides, the way I see it an early collar would get us off the street and down to Central Booking. No matter how chaotic Central Booking could get, not even a rookie could get you into trouble down there!

We stayed as close to the ground as possible as we made a run for the roof-landing door. Once in the staircase we wasted no time waiting for elevators, but instead took the stairs two at a time down to the lobby. It's a lot easier going down than up, and in no time at all we were racing out the back stairwell door towards Van Dyke Houses, and whoever it was up on that roof.

On our way out we interrupted a couple of young black teenagers who were finishing up a joint, who quickly changed their minds upon seeing two white cops coming toward them. Panicking, they tossed the partially smoked joint and ran out the back door, almost tripping over each other in the process. Once we had made it out of the building, I had all to do to keep the rookie from taking off down the street after the fleeing pot smokers.

While succeeding in pushing him in the general direction of Blake and Powell, I once again had all to do to restrain him from breaking into a full run. In a predominately black neighborhood where literally thousands of people are packed into a small area, it only takes the sight of a couple of white cops running down the street to precipitate a full scale riot. In no time at all you are guaranteed to have fifty to a hundred people running behind you. People who are anxious to see who the cops were chasing and more importantly, who they were gonna beat up! You never wanted to draw too much attention to yourself by running, which made it extremely difficult getting from one place to another on foot especially if you were in a hurry!

We quickly crossed Stone Ave, and once on the other side hurried along one of the several paved walkways that wove through the projects. As hard as we tried it was almost impossible not to attract some attention to ourselves as we passed several groups of individuals congregating in and around the various buildings.

Hanging out in a building's lobby, or for that matter merely in front of the building entrances, was an infraction of the project's regulations. Teenagers, upon seeing cops would immediately begin exiting lobbies and walking away from the front entrances. Their fear was that if they didn't move quickly enough they would be stopped and searched and if anything was found, regardless of the legality of the search, they would be arrested. And that was, unfortunately for them, an all too often reality.

The building we were headed for was off of Blake Avenue. However, the lobby did not face Blake Avenue but

34

instead faced the interior of the grounds, towards one of the smaller four story buildings.

Whether the rookie knew it or not we had ventured off our assigned post. More simply put we were not where we were supposed to be! Hopefully, whoever or whatever we ran into up on the roof would be worth the transgression. Going off your assigned post could get you into hot water, especially if things backfired. Fortunately, we hadn't attracted too much attention and the officer assigned to that particular post was nowhere to be seen. He had lucked out at roll call and hadn't been assigned a rookie. That, in and of itself, meant that he could be anywhere!

Having literally made a career of not being where I was supposed to be, I didn't even give it a second thought. In situations like this you acted on your instinct and you took your chances. You hoped that if the shit hit the fan you might still come up smelling like a rose if it wound up being a good collar. Although, in hindsight I really should have been a little more concerned about how this infraction could affect the rookie. Then again he had no choice in the matter, he had to do what he was told to do whether he wanted to or not. Hell, when you think about it, wasn't he the one who was itching for some action?

As we came through the lobby door of the Blake Avenue address, a couple of teenagers who hadn't initially seen us scampered for one of the rear doors. Ignoring them, we lucked out as an elevator was just arriving at the lobby level. We entered the elevator and just as the door was about to close, the teenagers who had only moments before fled upon seeing us tried to elbow their way onto the elevator, obviously wanting to follow us to see where we were going.

"Sorry guys," I said. "You'll have to take the next car, we're in a hurry there's a lady about to have a baby on the eighth floor!"

With that said the two would be passengers quickly lost interest and stepped back into the lobby. With that the elevator door closed. They probably didn't even live in the building but were ready to add to the chaos that might develop especially where cops were concerned.

They might still take the next car to see if we had gone to the eighth floor. Since that wasn't our destination, I couldn't have cared less. While I didn't have any intention of doing a number on whoever was up on the roof, should things get a little out of hand, I didn't need a couple of eye witnesses either. I am not big enough to be a violent person, and I had learned a long time ago that what people don't witness couldn't hurt them, and more importantly couldn't hurt me. I waited until after the door closed before I pushed the button for the 14th floor. Now all we had to do was hope and pray that the elevator didn't come to a stop between floors, an all too common occurrence in the projects.

Out of the corner of my eye I could see that the rookie had taken his memo book out of his back pocket and was opening it. He asked me what he should write, he apparently had picked up on the fact that we were off our assigned post.

It wasn't so much the question, but the way he had asked it that finally got to me. As the elevator arrived on the 14th floor and the door was sliding open I looked his way and said, "Do me a favor and put the fuckin' book away for now" and in the next breath, "When you get to the roof landing, stay inside until I signal you to come out. Got it?"

I'm thinking if whoever was up there is still there, it might not be a bad idea to watch him for a while to see what he's up to before we make our move.

We then both headed for the separate staircases leading up to the roof. As usual, the light bulb in my staircase was blown and no matter how many times you did it you never got used to ascending a blacked out staircase. You didn't dare use your flashlight unless you knew for certain that there was no one up there. A flashlight would alert anyone up there to the fact that you were on the stairs. In addition to the fact that the light could be seen from the roof, as there were windows at the top of the staircase. A lot of cops become complacent not realizing how dangerous staircases really are. And a lot of those cops are not around anymore.

I quietly entered the staircase making sure that I didn't let the door slam behind me. I removed my gun from my holster, and listened for less than a minute. Hearing nothing from above, I began climbing the steps one at a time straining to see in the darkness and hoping that the next step wasn't going to be my last!

# Chapter 11

**WHY WAS IT THAT AS FAR BACK** as he could remember, autumn had always been an unlucky time of year? He had been born in Detroit almost twenty-six years ago, the youngest of four sons born to Eula Mae Washington. His younger sister Nadine had been born right after Justin had turned five. All he remembered about his sister was her name. Three years after she was born, his mother had died. Relatives had told the boys that their mother had died in an automobile accident. Not having what could be considered a real father at the time; it wasn't very long after the funeral that the family had been split up. He and his brother Darryl had been shipped off to Mississippi to live with the family of his mother's oldest brother.

Uncle Lonnie had a little farm outside of Marks, a small town just north of Clarksdale. Compared to the housing projects in Detroit, the farm was a whole different world especially for two city bred boys. However, it didn't take too long for the novelty of life on the farm to wear off.

Justin's two other brothers, Billy and Vaughn had been sent to live with some cousins somewhere in Chicago.

Nadine being just barely three years old at the time remained in Detroit with Department of Child Welfare Services and he had heard that she was later adopted by some rich family.

Being only a little over a year apart in age he and Darryl became inseparable. They tended to keep their distance from Uncle Lonnie's sons who acted as if because of their father's owning the farm, they were somehow better than their cousins from Detroit.

Uncle Lonnie's wife, Hattie had to concern herself with not just her own six children but now her dead sister-in-law's two boys. Try as she did, there just wasn't enough money to go around, especially when it came to buying clothes for all the children. To help solve the problem she was always sewing, taking pants in and letting pants out.

 Being a good Christian woman she didn't mind doing for her newly acquired nephews. She just wished that they would show their appreciation a little more by doing their assigned chores around the farm, instead of running off to town all the time. She knew that her husband's patience with the two boys was slowly wearing thin. It seemed as if life on the farm just wasn't to their liking, never mind the fact that they constantly fought with Lonnie's older boys.

Both boys had had a few run-ins with the local Sheriff almost from the day that they arrived in Marks. They were constantly being picked up for getting into fights in town with other boys. The final straw was that Saturday afternoon when the two brothers had gone into town, ducking out on their chores around the farm.

Apparently, while walking around town they spotted two new bicycles that some boys had left outside a store. Darryl said that those boys deserved to get their bikes stolen, since they didn't bother to chain them up before going into the store. When Darryl said, "Let's you and me take those bikes." Justin didn't hesitate, and the next thing we did was run across the street where we each jumped on a bike and started peddling as fast as we could down the street toward the end of town. Justin peddled faster than Darryl and beat him out of town.

Having never once looked back, he didn't realize that Darryl was no longer behind him until he reached the dirt road that led to Uncle Lonnie's farm. He waited awhile, expecting to see Darryl ride up. When he didn't, he got scared and hid the bike in the woods. He ran the rest of the way to the farm, and hid up in the hay loft of the barn.

It was less than an hour later when he heard a car pull up the dirt road and stop in front of the house. Looking through some broken planks in one of the walls of the barn, he could see that it was a Deputy's car with Darryl sitting in the back seat. Justin could hear the Deputy telling Uncle Lonnie how he had seen Darryl in town with a bicycle whose chain had come off. Darryl, he said was trying to put the chain back on.

While he's talking to Darryl about how to fix the chain, a call comes over his police radio reporting the theft of two bicycles from in front of one of the stores in town. When the Deputy confronted Darry, he said that Darryl confessed and told him that it was Justin's idea to steal the bikes.

Justin couldn't believe what he was hearing; Uncle Lonnie listened to the Deputy and seemed to be getting angrier by the minute. The Deputy had finished up by tellin' Uncle Lonnie that if he could get Justin to just tell him where the other bike was he could then return it to the owner, and no charges would be filed against the boys.

Hearing this and being stupid enough to believe it, I decided to come down out of the hay loft before they came lookin' for me.

Uncle Lonnie angrily told me to go get the bike, tellin' me that nothing bad would happen as long as we gave the bike back. The Deputy waited while I ran down the road to get the bike and when I returned, he put the bike in the trunk of his patrol car. Then with a nod from Uncle Lonnie he threw me in the backseat with Darryl.

We were taken to the Police Station in town and locked in a cell. Later that day we were put back in a police car and taken to Clarksdale, where we were charged with stealing the bikes. Since Uncle Lonnie couldn't, or more likely wouldn't post the bond for our release, we were remanded to the County Detention Center for Wayward Minors.

# Chapter 12

**MEN AND WOMEN ALIKE ARE DRAWN** to careers in police work for any number of reasons. One of those reasons might be power; another might be job security, or even money. Then there are those who want to protect and serve those who can't protect themselves.

Some are very insecure individuals, who think that carrying a gun and wearing a badge will provide them with the strength that has eluded them thus far in their life. A magical strength that will help them function in an ever frightening and hostile world. For some of those individuals, at least in the beginning, they do find the strength and courage that they seek but it's only a temporary delusion. The first time they find themselves in a situation where it becomes necessary to call upon that courage, it just isn't there! Some of these unfortunate individuals, faced with such overpowering fears leave police work within the first year. Usually they find their niche in life doing something else.

The ones that don't quit wrestle with their fears for the next twenty years, at which time they put in their papers and retire. Once retired, they move to a warmer climate, and begin collecting their hard earned pension checks. It is usually within the first year or two, that they suffer a massive heart attack and die. The stress that caused that heart attack has been building up over the last twenty years.

As a cop, the individual reported for duty 4,400 times. During each and every one of those tours, he wondered if that was gonna be the one that got him killed.

Then there's the guy who always dreamed of donning the uniform and *walking a beat*, ideally because he cares about people and wants to make his city a safer and better place to live. This attitude usually goes right out the window the first time somebody knocks him on his ass. As a result, we now have a cop who will hit first and ask questions later. He will spend the next twenty years continually trying to justify his use of excessive force in almost every confrontation that he is involved in.

Strangely, a lot of cops are usually the guys who never gave going into police work any serious thought. A friend who was taking the police exam usually suggested that they also take the exam, just for the hell of it. In a lot of cases they passed the test and got the job, and the friend didn't. These are the cops that are the foundation of most departments. They report to work day in and day out, and do their job with a minimum of complaining. As long as they don't screw-up, down the road there's the promise of a pension..

I was an MP at the age of 17, got out of the service after serving three years and went on to become a cop. I luckily never got knocked on my ass, and as a result of several high profile arrests received 15 commendations. But then again, you could say that I was always a persistent type of guy.

Since I had failed the required 5' 8" height requirement on two separate occasions, I had to resort to lying flat on the floor of my uncle's living room for two days before the next physical. On that testing day I was driven to the academy, carried into the building, and up two flights of stairs on a makeshift stretcher by my uncle and some of his friends. At the last minute, I stood up and got on the height machine, and to the applause of the other candidates, measured up to the required 5' 8" necessary to become a police officer. Who knew at that time where my life was headed?

# Chapter 13

**AFTER SPENDING A COUPLE** of months at the detention center without any visitors we came to the conclusion that Uncle Lonnie had given up on us. We eventually went before a Judge and a small trial took place. Lookin' back now, it was more like a "kangaroo court". We were convicted on the word of the Deputy. There were no other witnesses and we never got to testify. The sentence was that we were to stay in the detention center until we reached our eighteenth birthday. Darryl, being a year older than me was released before me after having spent a little over three years locked up.

I made him promise that as soon as he could he would come back and help me escape. I wasn't going to spend another year locked up in that place. It wasn't that hard to escape from the detention facility but in order to do so, you need someone on the outside to help you.

It was a matter of maybe a month and a half before I was out, and me and Darryl was back together again.

His plan was that we head north to maybe New York. We didn't dare chance going back to Uncle Lonnie's place, because the cops would probably be watching there. We also had to worry about Uncle Lonnie, himself turnin' us in. He never visited us while we was locked up! When Darryl had gotten out and went to see him, his oldest sons ran him off the property. They told him that their father didn't want anythin' to do with him. They said that we caused his family enough trouble already!

So we headed north like Darryl had planned, hoping to eventually make it to New York City. One of the other inmates that we spent time with at the detention center was originally from New York. All he ever did was brag about how great it was up there.

We needed money to get there, so we robbed a few all night convenience stores along the way. That got us bus fare and some spending money. We used the pistol that Darryl had taken from one of the houses that we had broken into durin' our travels.

We only stuck up stores that were in out of the way places. By the time the owners were found beaten and tied up we'd be long gone, maybe already in the next state. Darryl would never hurt the store owners too badly, just hurt them enough so that they knew that we meant business.

After about a week of this, I started to notice a change in how Darryl treated me. He was becoming harder to get along with. He liked to think that only he knew how to rob places and because of that he started taking a bigger share of the money that we were stealin'; saying how bein' older entitled him to a bigger share. More than a few times when we were arguin' about the money, he'd pull out the pistol and point it right at my head sayin' how easy it would be to jest snuff me out, and keep all the money for hisself.

I wasn't sure about how much longer I could put up with his shit. After travellin' off and on for about a week, we wound up in some flea bag hotel in Baltimore, and the next morning boarded a bus for New York City. We got to New York and I guess that was when I made up my mind about killing Darryl

We got to the Port Authority bus terminal late in the afternoon, and being hungry we feasted on a couple of hot dogs with some sodas to wash them down.

After eatin' we headed over to the subway station on 42nd Street and Broadway. Darryl had the address of a guy who lived over in Brooklyn, and the plan was to go stay with him for a few days.

It wasn't as if I had really planned on doin' anythin' while we were standing there waiting for the train to pull in. But, because there were a lot of other people also waitin' for the train, Daryl and me were forced to stand close to the edge of the platform. I heard the roar of the train as it got closer and closer to us and how fast it was going really scared me. At the same time I thought to myself, "What the hell, why not!"

It only took a slight shove to send Darryl falling onto the tracks in front of the on-comin' train. He scared the shit out of me and a lot of other people too when he screamed, but that scream was quickly drowned out by the noise that the train made. Whoever was drivin' it must have really jumped on the brakes, as sparks on the tracks flew everywhere. But it was too late. The train's wheels had already cut Daryl in half!

I managed with all the confusion in the train station to edge my way through the crowd of screamin' women who had witnessed the accident. I was up the stairs of the station and on the street before anyone could have guessed that I was even involved. I would have liked to have seen the expression on Darryl's face just as he knew he was about to die. But he was turned away from me, trying to raise hisself up off the tracks. I guess we were now even, for that time back in Mississippi when he lied about me to the Deputy!

# Chapter 14

PERSONNEL ASSIGNED TO the Notification Desk are charged with contacting members of the force who need to be notified of impending promotions, transfers, and court appearances, in addition to anything else that the Patrol Bureau deems important. If they are unable to contact you during your scheduled working hours, they will call you at home. The individuals making the notification are under strict orders that they are not to pass the information on to anyone other than the officer, himself. In the past some members of the force apparently used the excuse that their wife forgot to tell them about a schedule change or a court appearance. Consequently, they couldn't be held accountable for not showing up.

I'd like a dollar for every notification that I have received over the past fifteen years. For the most part, they had to do with upcoming court appearances. When I saw the slip of paper that my wife had affixed to the door of the refrigerator telling me to call the Notification Desk, it didn't really faze me one way or another. However, after getting through to the Desk

SOME CALL IT JUSTICE

and being asked to hold on because the Lieutenant wanted to talk to me, alarms bells began to go off inside my head.


Lieutenant Mayer was one of the individuals who should have quit the job while he was still in the academy. He has been an embarrassment to the department for many years. He is tall with blond hair and grey eyes, and probably could have been an actor. He also looks good in uniform and probably made his parents very proud the day he graduated from the academy. He was also very impressed with himself, which was unfortunate. Being so narcissistic had apparently prevented him from ever attaining maturity, either professionally or personally.

During his early years as a police officer he had come to be known as somewhat of a coward. Not a nice reputation to have. He constantly managed to avoid dangerous situations by always being the last officer to arrive on the scene. He usually showed up as everyone else was about to leave, the situation having already been corrected. It was rumored that on a midnight to eight tour while on a foot post, he had heard a woman screaming. Instead of investigating and going to her aid, he had gone to a public telephone and called 911. He was definitely not the kind of cop that you wanted for a partner. However, he was a good student, and in less than five years, he had been promoted to Sergeant.

In the capacity of a supervisor, he showed up even less often. When he did, he constantly took to arguing with his subordinates threatening them with disciplinary action in order to insure their compliance. He eventually passed the lieutenant's exam, and that was when the CO of the patrol bureau finally decided that it was time to hide him somewhere. He was promptly tucked away in a small office at headquarters, where he couldn't do any damage. His job was to supervise the civilian employees who manned the telephones at the notification desk. His only hope of getting out of there was to do well on the captain's exam.

Consequently, he did nothing but study for the exam. He had no outside interests and his family was non-existent. His wife of seventeen years had left him, taking their two teenaged children with her. It seems, by his account that she had become romantically involved with another woman whom she had met while taking courses at the state university. He had actually bragged about this to anyone who would stand still for five minutes and listen. This man's ego was so big that it never dawned on him that he may very well have been the catalyst that drove his wife to abandon men and seek out women.

As a consequence of his new job his world had been reduced to a small cubicle where he surrounded himself with the study material for the captain's test. The few civilians that he supervised had their instructions. He was not to be disturbed under any circumstances, unless it was an absolute emergency,

While waiting for him to come on the line, I mentally prepared myself for the worst. We had commuted together from the Island for about six months, but we were not the best of friends. I automatically assumed that whatever it was that he had to tell me was not going to be good. He was probably enjoying every minute that he kept me waiting on the phone. After several minutes I had had enough and was about to hang up when he suddenly came on the line.

"Hey Cappy, Lieutenant Mayer here", he said.

Although it pained me to even have to answer, I said, "Yes sir"

"Hey Cappy, I've got some bad news for you. Effective 1200 this date. Your status as a detective was terminated and you are re-assigned to uniform patrol duties. Tough luck, kid! Listen, how soon can you get up here to headquarters? You need to turn in your gold shield, and pick up a patrolman's shield, and a new ID card. Oh, and by the way, you're scheduled for a midnight to eight tour over in Brownsville tonight.

"I'll probably be able to get up there sometime this afternoon. Thanks for the call", and before he could say anything further, I hung up. My boss had been the one who banished him into obscurity, a fact that he hadn't forgotten. He being able to tell me that I'd lost my gold shield, as far as he was concerned was almost like payback.

I had no intention of giving him the satisfaction of asking him, "What happened?" Although I had difficulty dialing the Inspector's private number, that's how upset I was.

# Chapter 15

**THE TELEPHONE WAS** usually answered by the Inspector himself, and if he had stepped out of the office for some reason or other, then his secretary would step into his office and answer it.

The fact that no one had picked up after a dozen rings was not very encouraging. Of course it didn't have to mean anything as he could be out of the office, and his secretary could be in the ladies room. I was almost in a panic by now, my mind raced frantically trying to think what I might have done to precipitate the demotion. Was the Inspector also somehow involved, and if so to what extent? What I was to discover was not only wasn't he in his office that afternoon, almost seven weeks ago; he wasn't even in the building. In fact, he was no longer even a member of the department! Such is the speed with which these things happen.

Apparently, getting rid of him had been in the works for quite some time. The only obstacle that had to be overcome was his very influential and powerful friends in the City's Jewish community. Inspector Campbell, whenever an opportunity presented itself, always went out of his way to accommodate these people, either with increased uniform patrols, or in some cases undercover teams to patrol their neighborhoods.

My partner and I were often sent to see a particular Rabbi or community leader. Our instructions were to listen to their complaints and assure them that the problem would be brought to the attention of the Inspector that very same day.

As we were leaving we told them that they could rest assured that Inspector Campbell would personally intervene and whatever it took to correct the situation would be done. Campbell knew that this individualized approach was a form of personal insurance for him, insulating him from the politics of City Hall.

Very few people would dare cross anyone who had friends in the powerful Hassidic community, with their large voting bloc. The Inspector's opponents were well aware of these friends, and the fact that any move against him would be immediately stopped by these religious leaders.

With very careful planning even the powerful can be toppled. His adversaries had discovered a way of accomplishing his removal with a minimum of political repercussions.

# Chapter16

I **COULDN'T BELIEVE** what I was hearing; here we are about to come up against some guy doing who knows what on the roof of a fourteen story building and the rookie wants to know, "What kind of memo book entry should I make?"

Maybe I shouldn't have come down on him as hard as I did, after all wasn't that the kind of shit that they were stressing in the academy these days. Hopefully, whatever the asshole on the roof was up to would be serious enough for an arrest and not just the issuance of a "C" summons. All I wanted was something to get me off the street with this rookie and down to central booking. That should kill a couple of hours and with any luck, by the time we get back to the Brownsville, it would be too late to return to patrol and we could call it a night.

The fact that the roof landing light was out and the stairwell was in total darkness came as no surprise, as light bulbs have a very short life expectancy in the projects. The local store owners will give the kids ten cents a bulb, and then turn around and sell them to unsuspecting customers for sixty cents apiece. It makes no difference how many times you've done it. You never got used to entering a pitch black stairwell. Never knowing what you'd find, you had to make as little noise as possible. After getting off the elevator on the 14th floor, I entered the stairwell leading to the roof, making sure that I didn't let the metal door slam behind me. It takes about a minute for your eyes to adjust to the darkness. I used that minute to listen for the sound of someone's heavy breathing. I knew that I was one hell of a target on the way up the narrow staircase, but I had no choice. I had to keep going. On this particular night, I already knew that there was at least one bad guy up on the roof. Most of the time that's not the case-you're the one at a disadvantage, climbing those cement stairs, one step at a time. With your gun in one hand and your nightstick in the other, you wondered if the next step that you took would be your last!

Housing cops assigned to foot patrol unlike their counterparts in PD, were rarely paired with another officer. You usually worked alone, and fifteen years ago when I came on the job, you didn't even have a radio with which to call for assistance. If you can picture what a flight of cement stairs looks like, you'll understand how there really isn't too much room with which to maneuver. This gets pretty serious if someone at the top decides to throw a few shots down in your direction. Believe me, it happens! Officers have been killed. Fortunately it doesn't happen too often. Taking that into consideration, a smart cop will always take checking roof landings very seriously assuming that there might be someone up there waiting to blow your head off, might just save your life someday.

# Chapter 17

CHIEF BENJAMIN PURDY an African-American had never risen above the rank of Lieutenant in PD. He was however, a committed student who while working as a cop, had managed to acquire a College Degree and a Law Degree. He was subsequently promoted by the Police Commissioner, on orders from City Hall to the position of Deputy Commissioner for Community Affairs. He was sent over to our Department to clean house, and that was indeed what he did!

They took seats facing the Chief's desk and waited. Inspector Campbell took one look at Purdy and knew immediately that this meeting was going to be anything, but routine. He and Purdy had already gotten off to a rocky start. Campbell had always felt that he had outranked Purdy. That was until he got his law degree, which was when he got the big appointment. Campbell always considered him nothing more than a glorified "lieutenant!"

After a perfunctory greeting, Purdy rudely returned to the stack of papers that he had been shuffling when they entered his office. He had never been known for his social graces, but this was a direct affront to the rank and position of both men seated across from him. It was obviously intended to demonstrate to them, once and for all, who exactly the boss was! Without bothering to look up, the Chief casually asked.

"Where would you two Captains like to be assigned?" Without waiting for a response, he continued,

"As of this moment, you are both hereby demoted to your former Civil Service rank of Captain."

Both men were speechless. The idea that a new boss, in order to establish his authority, would flex his muscles was understandable, but to do so in such a manner was inconceivable. In almost all large metropolitan police departments, the highest rank attainable through civil service competitive examination is Captain. Advancement beyond that involves a person being appointed to higher positions by the Chief of the Department. Conversely, when you are demoted it also is usually done by the Chief, and you can't be reduced below your highest Civil Service rank. If circumstances warranted a further reduction in rank, in all likelihood there also would probably exist grounds for dismissal, or even arrest.

The Inspector, putting it mildly was beside himself, and stormed out of the Chief's office muttering under his breath, "We'll see about this!"

In addition to the humiliation of being demoted in rank and becoming subordinate to individuals who clearly held him in contempt, was the amount of money that he stood to lose because of what the Chief had just done. The reduction in pay alone would amount to well over $18,000.00 dollars a year. Campbell hurried back to his office and left orders with his secretary that he was not to be disturbed under any circumstances. With the door securely closed, he sat behind his desk, picked up his phone and started dialing his "friends". He wanted to reach them before the situation got out of hand and possibly beyond their control. After ten minutes of trying to reach several very influential Rabbis with no success the realization that he had been "had", finally settled in. That particular Monday, unfortunately for him, was one of the most revered of Jewish holidays. Both Orthodox, and in particular Hasidic Jews, are forbidden by tradition from doing certain things on that day. One of the prohibited acts was, *talking on the telephone!*

Thus, Inspector Richard Campbell's career of almost thirty years of police service had ended.

The Deputy Chief, being a more likable person, did manage to find a friendly ear at City Hall and as a favor to him; a call was made to the Chief from someone in the Mayor's office instructing him to hold off on the demotions until noon. That small reprieve, gave both Campbell and the Deputy Chief enough time to submit their retirement papers. This allowed them the benefit of a pension based on their respective ranks of Deputy Chief and Inspector.

# Chapter 18

**REACHING THE TOP OF** the stairs and not finding anyone there, I crouched down in front of the door and carefully pushed it open just far enough to be able to see the roof itself. I had purposely taken the staircase on my right as we exited the elevator, directing the rookie to take the left staircase. That put me closest to where I had last seen the perp moving about. From my position behind the door, I could still see a figure over in the far corner of the roof. I still couldn't tell what he was up to, so I decided to just watch him for a couple of minutes before confronting him.

One minute he was standing, and his figure was outlined against the evening sky. The next minute he was gone from view as he lowered himself below the top of the brick parapet. It was now getting later and darker by the minute. I had turned off my radio before entering the stairwell not wanting it to go off un-expectantly and thereby announcing my presence and it was still off. I cursed myself for not making sure that the rookie had done the same.

It soon became apparent that he hadn't, when the sound of Central calling another unit could be heard loud and clear from where O'Brien was himself waiting for my signal.

Our "friend" had undoubtedly also heard the radio, and in a matter of seconds was once again in view. This time though, he's coming toward the door behind which I am crouched.

I was instantly on my feet pushing the door fully open and with my gun pointing directly at his chest, bringing him to a sudden stop!

His eyes seemed to bulge a little, with his mouth agape, as he was less than a three feet from the business end of my 38 S&W service revolver.

"On the ground asshole, face down" I shouted, cocking my gun to emphasize the point. As he got to the ground, I added, "Spread your arms and legs outward!"

Unlike TV police shows, most of the cops that I know, including me would rather not get into a fight with the person they are trying to arrest. . A lot of the bad guys, at least in my case, are usually bigger than me. In addition to the fact that it's not very safe to have to wrestle the perps to the ground, there's always the chance that you might get hurt in the process. Unfortunately, with some of perps you just can't help getting physical. They're trying to kick your ass, and you have to defend yourself. Months down the road, a Review Board will examine your actions and make a determination as to whether or not you used too much force in making the arrest.

How much force is too much, when you are trying to convince someone that he should come with you peacefully? Sometimes you're rolling around on the ground with him, as he tries to rip your gun from your holster.

If you hit him over the head with your nightstick, how hard should you swing?

What if you don't swing hard enough and it does nothing but really piss him off! What do you do then, shoot him? I don't know too many fellow officers who will just stand there and let the asshole get his kicks in, but if you listen to the bleeding heart liberals, that's exactly what they expect you to do. Like I've said, the TV cops don't have to concern themselves with such bullshit and neither should we!

An old timer once gave me some advice that has come in handy on a number of occasions. If you should ever find yourself in a really scary situation, he told me. "Like maybe on the roof of a fourteen story high riser, face to face with an asshole who's a lot bigger than you, and it doesn't look like he wants to cooperate", his advice was to just start acting as scared as hell!

"Point your gun at him", he said, "and begin shaking like a bastard. It tends to scare the shit out of them!"

The criminals know just how far a cop can go. They know for example, that a cop can't just shoot them without justification. Point your gun at someone in an arrest situation who hasn't pulled a gun or a knife, and you are likely get told by the really hard cases, "Why don't you just shove that gun up your ass?"

On the other hand, start shaking that same gun in some asshole's face while appearing to be really terrified, and you'll soon discover that you now have a truly terrified individual. He doesn't know whether to shit or go blind.

He's scared that you might accidently shoot him, which would make him just as dead, as if you intended to kill him in the first place!

He'll probably start to say things like, "Take it easy now officer, I'm cool, I'm cool, Just arrest me. Please, please be careful with that gun. Please....."

This guy on the ground wasn't all that big. He may have been a couple of inches taller than me, but I'm sure I outweighed him by at least thirty pounds. That put him on the tall and skinny side. Once on the ground, spread eagled, all I had to do was keep the big barrel of my gun pointed at his head. He knew that the gun was cocked, so I had his undivided attention. I ordered him to place his hands, one at a time behind his back He complied and I cuffed him.

Out of the corner of my eye I saw a small figure running towards me. Thinking that this could be an accomplice, I almost fired a round at the advancing figure. I held my fire at the very last moment when I realized that it was a very young girl. I ordered her to stand still and began shouting for the rookie, remembering that I had told him to stay put until I called for him. In an instant I heard the other roof door slamming, and see O'Brien's running to where I'm now standing over the prisoner, with my gun still pointed at him.

Still not sure of exactly what we had, I tell O'Brien to cover our friend, while I walk the young girl a short distance away. Near enough to be able to keep both the perp and O'Brien insight, but far enough so that what the girl was saying could not be overheard.

She was a small frail looking kid and didn't look more than six or seven years old. She was wearing blue jeans that appeared to be partially torn in front, where her zipper had been. She held a small pair of sneakers in one hand, and was attempting to hold up her jeans with the other.

There was some dried blood at the corner of her mouth. She was shaking uncontrollably, and softly crying at the same time. I had my hands full just trying to convince her that I wasn't going to hurt her, such was her state of fear. After I was able to calm her down, she told me that her name was Azzurinthia, and that she lived nearby in one of the low rise buildings. When I asked her how old she, she replied, "twelve", something that I initially found difficult to believe. As gently as I knew how, I asked her what had happened. She again became emotional, and between the crying and fearful glances over to where the perp was face down under the watchful eyes of O'Brien, she related the following:

Our cuffed friend had approached her while she was playing on the corner, having just come down from watching TV. He asked her if she could help him find a lady who lived in this building, possibly he said on the fourteenth floor. He told her that he had found a bottle of medicine that belonged to that lady and he wanted to return it to her. He then showed her the medicine bottle, and after she agreed to help him, they both began walking toward the building. She got on the elevator with him and they rode up to the top floor.

Once off the elevator, instead of walking towards the apartment doors, he lifted her off her feet and took her into the stairwell. Cupping his hand over her mouth, he forced her to climb the stairs, threatening to kill her if she tried to scream. Once out on the roof, he forced her to look over the parapet to the ground below. He told her that if she didn't do exactly what she was told; he'd throw her off the roof. He made her take off her sneakers and then pulled her jeans down. When she began to struggle, her smacked her across the mouth. Once he had her jeans down around her ankles, he ripped off her panties.

At that point in her story, she once again began crying un-controllably. Based on just what she told me thus far, I had a felonious assault and an attempted rape. Whether he could also be charged with the kidnapping would depend on what the District Attorney's office decided.

I switched my portable radio back on and called Central.

"Tilden Unit 2746 to Central K" I said

"Proceed 2746" came the reply.

"Central be advised that I have one male under arrest on the roof of 420 Blake Ave., as well as one female victim of an assault. I need a unit to meet me on Blake and Powell for transportation of the prisoner to PSA 2".

"10-4, Unit 2746." I then heard central asking.

"What unit available to respond to Blake and Powell to 10-85 Unit 2746 for transport of a 10-12"

At that point several units answered up, and the anti-crime unit said they were closest and enroute forthwith!

I walked the short distance over to where O'Brien was guarding the prisoner.

"I just advised Central that we need transportation" I said to O'Brien and continued,

"Let's get him downstairs, they're meeting us on Blake and Powell"

"Should we take one of the elevators?" asked O'Brien.

"No, we better take the stairs. I don't want to run into any friends he might have on the way down." I replied.

With that, we each grabbed an arm and lifted the now protesting prisoner to his feet. He kept saying that we were hurting him, that the cuffs were too tight. With the little girl trailing, we headed for the roof-landing door that only minutes earlier I had been crouched behind.

Foregoing the elevators we began the trek down fourteen flights of stairs. Once safely outside the building, the scumbag kept trying to get the little girl's attention by calling her sweetheart and honey.

Seeing this I said, "You say one more word to that child, and I swear, I split your head open! You got that?" He mumbled something under his breath, but he didn't say anything further to the child. None-the-less, I shoved his face within two inches of the brick wall of the building, and knowing that the car was on its' way, I used this time to advise him of his rights.

"Listen up pal! You got the right to remain silent; anything you say can be used against you. Do you understand? OK, so just shut up!"

# Chapter 19

POLICE OFFICERS LaROSA and Shea drove their unmarked department vehicle right up onto the sidewalk, coming to a stop within ten feet of where we stood.

Jim LaRosa and Billy Shea had been on the job a little over five years. Both cops were very active in their respective fraternal organizations. La Rosa being of Italian descent was a Columbian, and Shea was a member of the Emerald Society. They both had strong "hooks" who had convinced someone that these two young officers had a lot of potential.

The word had been passed down to their Captain, and they were subsequently assigned to a special anti-crime plainclothes detail. Their job in that assignment was to distinguish themselves. It was a nice little detail, steady 4 to 12, with Sundays and Mondays off. I had met them for the first time six weeks earlier when I had been re-assigned to uniform. They were given one of the old unmarked cars to use. They even had their own little office off to the right just as you entered PSA 2. They couldn't care less that it had once been an oversized mop closet. To them, it was their "office" even though it was only big enough to accommodate a small table, a folding chair, and a small stool. Looking back it's still a lot more than my partner and I started out with, doing pretty much what they're doing now.

They had a reputation of being greedy for collars, and that they would take anything they could get their hands on. As far as they were concerned, every collar that they could make was that much closer to a detective's gold shield. They already had the "hooks", and I'm sure that they were told that all they needed was some really "high numbers" to get them into the Detective Bureau.

La Rosa and Shea had picked up the call from Central for the 10-85 on Blake and Powell. While it was obvious that the rookie and I had the situation under control with the perp cuffed, and facing the wall. Shea, none-the-less, felt it was necessary to draw his gun as he approached us, and almost tripped over his own feet in the process.

La Rosa was a little more "cool" about the whole thing; however the first words out of his mouth were,

"Do you want the collar?" I guess they had discussed how to approach the situation while driving over, and decided that it would probably be better if La Rosa were to ask for the collar, rather than Shea. You know one "eyetalian" to another.

Asking whether I wanted the collar or not, was the last thing I expected to hear at that moment. While I really knew very little about these two cops, it was obvious that they probably still believed in Santa Claus as well as the Tooth Fairy!

Who in their right mind would ever give up a collar like this? I mean, some shithead with a stolen car battery, it's all yours my friend! But an Attempted Rape on a small child, not in their wildest dreams! Maybe the Pope, back when we had an Italian one, maybe, just maybe, he could have talked me into giving up this one.

If these two hot shots spent more time working the street, and less time sitting at Dunkin Donuts flirting with the cute servers, maybe the cuffs that our prisoner was sporting behind his back, just might have been theirs instead of mine.

Conspicuously ignoring La Rosa's question about the collar I said.

"Do me a favor and take the rookie and the prisoner back to the PSA."

"Where you goin?" asked La Rosa.

"I'm gonna walk the kid over to where she said she lives. I'll explain it all to her parents. They're gonna need to accompany the kid to the hospital for the medical exam. After that we'll be able to decide what to charge the scumbag with." I said.

"How you gonna get to the hospital?" asked Shea.

"Don't worry about it; I'll call Central from the kid's apartment, once I finish up with the parents." I said.

I'd planned to have a car pick me and the parents up. They could then drop me off at the PSA before heading to the hospital for the medical exam. I didn't feel that it was important for me to be there.

Those officers could take custody of whatever medical evidence was obtained. I wanted to get back to the prisoner; I didn't like the idea of him sitting there with a rookie all by himself.

For the first time in the last seven weeks, my luck seemed to be taking a turn for the better. Hopefully, with this collar, things would start to improve.

The little girl lived with her mother and two older sisters in one of the smaller buildings in the projects. These smaller building were situated here and there throughout the complex providing variety to the otherwise concrete jungle. They were only three stories high, with six apartments per floor. It turned out that she lived on the second floor of 263 Blake Avenue, a short distance from where the bastard had grabbed her. One of her sisters came to the door and said that their mother had gone shopping, and would probably be back in a little while. The little girl had scooted past her older sister, and having no other choice but to wait, I followed her into the small apartment. The first thing that caught my eye was the absence of any real furniture. There was only a beat up old couch against one wall of the living room facing a black and white TV set that was propped up on an empty plastic milk crate. Seeing a telephone on the kitchen wall, I decided to give

Central a call and let them know what was going on. As I entered the kitchen I noticed a dog attached to a leash that was tied to a nearby radiator eating left over food from a bowl. I was glad to see that its' attention was on the bowl of food and not on me. From the look of the animal, with its' ribs straining against the thin skin of its belly, taking a bite out of my leg wouldn't have been too far from its thoughts. Plus, I know for a fact that dogs aren't impressed with police uniforms; although by all accounts we do seem to impress them more than mailmen. While it is strictly forbidden by the rules and regulations of the city housing authority to have dogs or even cats for that matter, many tenants will keep a dog for protection. The project managers look the other way, as long as the dogs don't create too much of a nuisance.

I got the dispatcher for the Brownsville Complex on the phone and brought him up to speed. I gave him the address of where I was, and he said he would dispatch another car to my location.

It doesn't take very long for news to travel through a housing project. Someone had seen me enter the building with the little girl and had been curious enough to find out what apartment I had gone to. Eventually the mother who had been shopping over on Belmont Avenue heard that a cop was at her apartment, and that it had something to do with her younger daughter. Not more than five minutes had passed since I entered the apartment before the mother burst through the front door, completely out of breath wanting to know what was going on.

The mother seeing her daughter and the condition of her clothing got upset. It took me a couple of minutes to calm her down, at least enough so that I could explain to her what had happened. While all of this is going on, the daughter is quietly sitting on the couch watching TV. Either the volume didn't work or it was turned all the way down as I could hear no sound what-so-ever. Moments later, two other uniformed officers showed up at the door. I went on to explain to the mother how important it was that we get her daughter to the hospital and that the two officers were here to take them. On the way out of the apartment I asked her if someone would be contacting her husband, and she replied that she didn't have a husband. That the child's father had run out on her about six years ago. That sort of thing was not that unusual in the projects, I've heard it time and time again.

# Chapter 20

**I STILL CAN'T BELIEVE WHAT'S** happenin', one minute it's just me and the little girl havin' a good ole time, and the next minute, I gots a cop pointin' a gun at me. How could he have seen me? I know no one was up here when I brought the girl up to the roof! Now here I is, lying face down, with my hands cuffed behind my back.

Of all the stupid shit I've done in my life, gettin' caught like this has to be the worst. How the hell am I gonna get outta this one?

The short fat cop, the one that grabbed me, hell, if he hadn't had that gun of his stuck up in my face, I probably could a kicked his ass. The other cop, the young one, hell, he acts like a real pussy, tellin' me not to get so mad, that this is probably all a big mistake. He says he's sorry, but he can't take the cuffs off me cause he doesn't wanna get the other cop mad. I was sure that he had believed me when I told him that I was only tryin' to help the little girl find the guys that beat her up.

The young cop, after the other one had walked off a ways with the little girl, up and introduced hisself, tellin me his name is Bill. I had the urge to tell him, "What do I give a shit what your name be. I jest want you to take these cuffs off me, and let me get outta here!", but I didn't say anythin'.

I was sure that I had the young cop belivin me. I would never have let them put the cuffs on me if I hadn't thought there was a chance that they was gonna let me go. After all, I did cooperate with them, didn't I?

I could see the little bitch over in the corner with that other cop, whimperin' and cryin' like she didn't like what we was doin'. I knowed that I should have thrown her off the roof the minute she started carryin' on. This is the thanks I gets for bein' a nice guy and not hurtin' her all that much.

Now the fat one is talkin on his walkie talkie. Shit, I bet he's callin for help. That's it, they got me now, they jest aint gonna lets me go! Now he's walkin' back over here again. I jest wish they would go ahead and jest kill me! I aint goin back to jail again! The fat one tells the other cop to grab an arm and they pull me to my feets. He then tells me that we're goin down the back stairs nice and quiet like. He whispers in my ear that if I so much as flinches the wrong way, he's gonna blow my balls off!

Then to make sure I believes him, he points his gun at my crouch and cocks it! He thinks he's a bad ass with that gun and badge. Jess takes off these cuffs for one minute, and I'll show them that they can't mess with Justin Washington and get away with it. I guess I gotta jest play along with them for now, and wait until I gets my chance, then I'll shows them.

We finally make it outside, having come through the back door of the buildin'. The fat one makes me stand with my face against the brick wall of the building, so I can't see what's goin' on behind me. Some peoples musta walked over to see what was happenin', because the fat one tells em to leave, that it's none of their business. The next thing I know he is readin' me my rights, only he's not readin' from anything, he gots it all memorized and everythin'. What am I supposed to be impressed or somethin'? He finishes by tellin me to "shut up"! Well I aint sayin nothing.

I hear the siren of a police car getting closer and closer and all of a sudden a car pulls up on the sidewalk. I go to turn around to see who it be, and the fat cop tells me, "don't turn around".

One of the cops that just pulled up calls the fat cop, Cappy. He asks him if he wants the collar? Shit, what do they think I is and animal? They already got me in cuffs, now they want to put a collar around my neck. This Cappy cop, he don't answer, he just tells these other cops to take me and the rookie, I guess that be Bill, to the police station, that he'll be there in a little while.

"Hey man, you don't gotta shove me, I can walk", I tells the tall one who just got there, and is already pushing me to the car. I ask him,

"Where we goin?" and he says,

"Just shut up asshole!"

"Who you tellin' to shut up? You white honky!" I says to him.

With that, the bastard takes hold of the cuffs behind my back that are already tight as hell, and squeezes them even tighter, cutting off my circulation. Already I feel my hands getting' numb. Just wait, I thinks to myself. You have to take these cuffs off sooner or later, and when you do, I'll be ready. You just better hope you are too.

The fat cop, Cappy, aint comin with us and it's just as well, cause I don't knows how we would have all fit in this car.

The tall one, who aint drivin, gets on the radio and tells Central, that we're comin in. I guess that means that they're takin' me to the police station.

The two cops in the front seat are talkin kinda low, and I can't make out what they be sayin. All I could catch was the words, "lucky old bastard". They sound mad about something, and they not payin' us no mind in the back seat.

We pull up in front of the police station, and the two cops up front don't even bother getting' out of the car. It's almost like they don't give a shit what happens anymore. They tell Bill to jest takes me inside and the Sarge will tell him what to do.

I figure now is my chance; even with the cuff on I could probably outrun Bill.

I gots to time it just right, and hope the police car pulls away before we gets inside the front door.

We gets out of the car, Bill is behind me, and I'm in luck, as Bill's not even botherin' to hold onto my arm!

The police car makes a right turn at the corner, and disappears down Hinsdale. We're about ten feet from the from door, and I'm jest getting ready to make a run for it, when two other cops, one white and one black, come walkin' out the door of the police station. The white one I know I could beat in a race, but the black one I'm not so sure. We brothers are pretty fast, and he looked like he could move pretty quickly. The white one holds open the door, so me and Bill could go through without skipping a beat!

Once inside, Bill tells the sergeant what happened and that Cappy will be in shortly. The sergeant tells Bill to take me into one of the back rooms and wait for Cappy.

In the room is a small table and a couple of chairs. There's a mirror on one wall that I know is one of those one-way see through jobs. Bill tells me to sit in one of the chairs, and when I motion for him to take the cuffs off, he again apologizes, sayin he doesn't have the key, that Cappy will take them off when he comes in.

I tell him that I have to go to the bathroom, and he answers, "Later".

A couple of minutes go by and I again tell him that I have to use the bathroom, figurin' this is the only way I'm ever gonna get these cuffs off. He again says, "Later".

"Later, what?" I tell him. "I gots to take a shit now!"

I guess he's just not gonna take these cuffs off of me. I must have told this cop at least a dozen times that I had to go to the bathroom. "You aint gonna be happy till I shits my pants", I told him.

We been sittin in this office for almost an hour now, and every time I asks him to take the cuffs off he tells me he aint got the key. Who do he think he be bull shittin'? I try to stare his ass down, but he jest looks away. The son of a bitch has been readin' the newspaper now for the last twenty minutes.

Who is I kiddin'? Even if he took the cuffs off, and I managed to get a jump on him with a real good kick to the balls, I'd still have to get his gun and shoot the bastard. There's got to be at least a dozen more cops out there who'd hear the shot and come runnin' in. I knows I could get another two or three before they got me, but I sure as hell would never make it outta the building alive. Not a good idea. Maybe I'll just sit tight and see what happens, I is really not ready to die yet. I don't wanna go to prison, at least not if I can help it. Maybe we could work out a deal, my lawyer and the Judge. I could plead out to some lesser charge, and maybe skate with some probation for a sentence.

If I end up in prison and word gets out and it usually do, that I did a kid I'd be finished! You could shoot the Pope and nobody would give a shit cept maybe some religious Puerto Rican, but you mess with a kid and them cons will cut your balls off, and shove them so far down your throat that you'll wind up choking to death.

SOME CALL IT JUSTICE

# Chapter 21

**WHY, I THINK TO MYSELF,** did I ever agree with Darryl to come to this shit hole of a city? I aint had nothin but bad luck from the get go!

Shit, I wasn't even eighteen when Darryl and me got off that bus all them years ago, and everythin' has gone downhill ever since then.

The first couple of weeks had been a blast, what with the beach and all. Then being sent to prison for all those years, after I got shot during the stick-up, was almost like diein' and goin' to hell.

After I finally get out, I wind up getting' hooked up with the bitch, Darlene.

Again, things started to go bad after the kid died, and I spent another year behind bars.

When I finally talk her into changin' her story, and they let me out, I had made up my mind to head back down south. "No", Darlene says. "Up here we're blacks, down south; we're still just niggers!" So I stay here and look at what happens to me now.

Thinkin back, I remember the feelin' of knowin that I was finally my own boss and I was livin' in the biggest city in the world. I had managed to con Darryl into letting me hold onto the pistol, once we had gotten into the city. Since I was young, I probably wouldn't be searched if anythin' ever went wrong. He wasn't buyin' partin' with any of the money so when I pushed him onto the tracks, I also pushed what little money we had left from the stick-ups, which totaled $78.00. I had to come up with some money and it was gonna have to be real soon. I was already startin' to feel hungry.

Darryl had taught me how to roll drunks for some chump change, nickels and dimes and I still had the pistol that I could use if I had to. We had been to a few cities on our way up north, some big and some small. In the smaller ones you had to be careful because strangers stood out and got the attention of the cops. They were only too happy to rent you one of their jail cells.

When we got to the Big Apple, you had to forget about small town ideas cause there were dudes who could spot you a mile away and who were experts at separatin' you from whatever you owned, regardless of its' value.

It was a local pastime for these slick dudes, just like huntin' and fishin' were pastimes for Uncle Lonnie's boys.

After the thing with Darryl, I spent the first couple of days and nights roamin' the streets, and stealin' from drunks that I came across passed out in alleys. I spent what little money I got on potato chips and Twinkies, washin' it all down with Pepsi's. Since the weather was still warm, I could sleep during the day in the big park in the city without havin' to worry about anybody botherin' me.

I even made it to a place called Coney Island. I had fallen asleep on the subway and woke up at the last stop which is where I discovered this big amusement park. The place was great, plenty of beaches and a boardwalk that I could sleep under if I didn't want to ride all the way back to the city. Only problem was that I had to get back to the city every couple of days, so I could make some money to buy food.

Once the weather started to turn chilly at night, I decided to step up my money making, so I could maybe find a place to sleep that was indoors.

I decided to hit on liquor stores and the first one I stuck-up, turned out to be my last!

Decidin' to use the pistol that I had been carryin' around since getting into the city, I cased me a liquor store in the mid-town Manhattan area over on the West Side. I watched from a nearby alley until the place was empty, cept for the owner, who looked like he was getting ready to close for the night.

Before he could lock the front door, I managed to walk in and put the pistol right up in his face threatenin' to blow his brains out unless he gave me all the money he had. He gave it all up, and once I had it, I decide to lock him in the bathroom that was in the back of the store. Up to that point everythin' had gone like clockwork. I had put the gun back in my pocket and walked back out to the front of the store, countin' the money on the way. I guess I hadn't heard them come in the store and before I knew what was happenin' someone shouts "Merry Christmas, mother fucker!" The son of a bitch shoots me!

Don't ask me how I lived through that one, cause those cops meant business. I think they was sure that I was gonna die, cause one of them tells the other, "He's a goners, no sense wastin' another bullet on him"

I found out later that I had to get six pints of blood at the hospital, which is really what saved my life.

About a week later, the Judge and all came to the hospital to press charges against me, as I couldn't leave the hospital yet. It took almost a month before I was strong enough to go to court. Well, I coulda saved the trip because those two cops lied their heads off on the stand. They said that I refused to drop my pistol, and that they shot me in self-defense after having identified themselves as policemen. They really took the gun outta my pocket while I was on the floor, almost dead.

Then the cops took the cash I had taken from the store and I guess it was after that is when they called an ambulance, and I was taken to the Hospital.

The Judge appointed me one of those Legal Aid lawyers, and he told me that I was in a whole shit-load of trouble, facing maybe twenty years in prison. The cops were chargin' me with Armed Robbery and Attempted Murder of a Police Officer. My only chance accordin' to him was to plead guilty to Robbery in the second degree to cover all the charges. Being a first offender, I would probably not get more than 7 ½ to 15 years, and with good behavior, I'd probably be out in 5 years.

It was funny the way it was done. My lawyer had told me that he had talked to the Judge, and the Judge said that he was goin' to go easy on me. When I got up before the Judge, before they accepted my guilty plea, the Judge asks me if I was pleadin' guilty cause I was guilty and I had to answer yes. He then asked me if anyone had made any promises to me in exchange for my pleadin' guilty, and I was jest about to repeat what my lawyer said to me when the little bastard pokes me in the ribs and says, "Say no", so I says, "No"

Well, all's I know is that I spent a little over four years in a place upstate called Coxsackie, and boy was it cold in the winter time! The place was really overcrowded, but as long as you were cool nobody really messed with you. I sometimes wonder if the Parole Board ever took into consideration the fact that I had taken a bullet in the stomach and lost half of it on the operating' table.

That was six years ago, and it wasn't long before Darlene and me hooked up. She was getting her ass kicked by her pimp one night and I stopped him from cuttin' her up with a razor. We been together ever since, both thru good times and thru bad.

# Chapter 22

**IT ISN'T TOO OFTEN THAT** a police officer is lucky enough to catch someone committing a sex crime. These are typically crimes of opportunity where the criminal picks the time and place, and they often occur behind closed doors or in an out of the way place. In fifteen years of police work I can recall only one other time that I had actually come upon a sex crime in progress, and while it's been over ten years ago, it's an arrest that I'll never forget.

While walking a foot post, working a 12 X 8 tour in uniform, I stumbled across a middle aged woman leaning out of her second floor apartment window. Being 3 AM, even in Brownsville, it aroused my curiosity.

Upon seeing me in uniform on the sidewalk nearby, she began frantically waving her arms, obviously trying to get my attention. As I approached the building to see what the problem was, she began to excitedly point down into the small parking area that was almost directly under her window. As I headed to where she was pointing, I could clearly hear a woman sobbing. The crying was coming from inside of one of the parked vehicles. The car in question upon closer inspection, didn't appear to have any wheels, and was propped up on four metal milk crates.

While it was obviously an abandoned vehicle, it certainly appeared to be occupied at the moment. There was a black male in the front seat who was turned around facing the rear. He seemed to be reaching into the back seat where he appeared to be holding down the shoulders of a young black female. Another black male who was in the back seat, was straddling the female while holding her legs apart, and forcing her to engage in sexual intercourse. They had apparently smacked her around before I had gotten there, and her screams are what attracted the other woman to the window. Being by myself I drew my weapon, and ordered both men out of the car at gunpoint. I was ready to shoot the first one that tried anything. One of them kept saying that everything was cool, and that she was his girlfriend. However, when I asked him her name, his answer was, "Ask her yourself." After cuffing the two, I asked the female to step out of the car.

After having beaten her pretty badly about the face, they had taken turns raping her. She told me that she had met the two men in a bar on Sutter Avenue several hours earlier, and that they had bought her a couple of drinks. When the bar finally closed, they had asked her if she wanted to go to a party. Since they had been so nice to her, she decided to accept the invitation. After getting into what she thought was their car and then realizing that they weren't driving away, it became obvious to her that she was going to be "the party." When she tried to get out, they got real nasty and started to punch her in the face, threatening to kill her. The beatings ended only after she stopped resisting and let them have sex with her.

Frequently, in sex crimes an arrest is only made after an extensive investigation is conducted. Sometimes an arrest may never be made if the police haven't any leads to follow with which to help identify the rapist. In a lot of situations where the victim and the rapist are unknown to each other and where we don't have any witnesses, aside from hoping for a break, there really isn't too much that can be done.

Fortunately, for the young lady in the above situation a concerned citizen went to her window when she heard the screams. That I just happened to be walking my beat at that moment in time resulted in an arrest. Whether they would have killed her after having had their way, is a question that thank God we didn't have to deal with. In March 1964, many years earlier in a quiet neighborhood in Kew Gardens, Queens, a woman named Kitty Genovese wasn't as fortunate. She died at the hands of her attacker.

# Chapter 23

BY THE TIME THE GUYS who were taking the victim and her mother to the hospital, dropped me off at the station house it was already going on six thirty; over forty-five minutes had elapsed since we'd arrested the shithead on the roof.

Apparently word had spread pretty quickly among the cops on patrol. As I walked into the PSA there were a couple of black officers standing just inside the entryway. As I passed them one said, "Nice collar, Cappy!" while another added, "Great work man!"

Quite a few of the black cops assigned to PSA 2 grew up in neighborhoods like Brownsville, and some of them still lived in the surrounding areas. When a young child is sexually molested, all of us who have children, especially daughters, put ourselves in the shoes of the parents. It hits the black cops even harder than the rest of us. Unlike most white cops who live in the suburbs, the black officers living in the city, can't help but feel that it could have just as easily been their daughter who was molested.

Contrary to what the public has come to believe, a significant number of black officers don't take too kindly to seeing their black "brothers" being arrested, especially by white cops when it comes to petty crimes, like loitering, gambling, disorderly conduct, and the occasional pot smoker. These individuals are not looked upon as criminals by most of your average black officers, and they resent it when white officers make these kinds of arrests.

However, when it comes to serious crimes like, murder, rape, robbery, burglary, and arson; black officers are known to react even more vigorously than their white counterparts, because it is usually their neighbors who are the victims.

Then again there are the Officer LaRosas and Shea's of the world. What really pissed them off more than anything else that night is that someone else and not them had made the collar!

They look at things believing that luck plays a big part in making good collars. That just being out there isn't enough unless you get lucky. I'll concede that there is a certain amount of luck involved in stumbling across a crime in progress, but what they seem to totally discount is the fact that you have to be out there before luck can even come into play.

After acknowledging the compliments from several cops, I approached the Desk. Sergeant O'Leary, the boss who only hours earlier had put the screws to me by assigning me a rookie, had gone out on patrol. He probably went looking for me! He had been replaced by Lieutenant Romano, who had what can only be described as a shit eating grin on his face when he said,

"You did it again! Nice piece of police work, Cappy."

"Thanks Lou, any idea where the rookie's been stashed with the prisoner?" I asked.

"I told him to take the prisoner back to the administrative lieutenant's office," he replied, adding,

"I figured he'd be safer there than in one of the holding cells. The word is probably out all over the neighborhood by now and I certainly don't want any angry citizens trying to take the law into their own hands. Anybody asks me, the prisoner already left for Central Booking."

"Good thinking, boss!" I said. Lieutenant Romano, while not being much of a cop, was actually a really nice guy, that's about the best way to describe him. He very rarely spoke above a whisper. His timidity with dealing with people was legendary throughout the job. He rose through the ranks, making sergeant in six years, and lieutenant four years later. Having never made that many collars, he wasn't what you would call a "street cop".

In the Housing Police, just as in any other police department, good collars were rewarded with commendations. These commendations carried with them numerical points, which could be applied to promotional exams. This had the effect of increasing your test scores, which would put you higher on a promotional list. The higher you were on the list, the faster you were promoted. Another plus when it came to promotions was having been in the military as veteran's credits also carried points. Since Romano lacked the collars he didn't have the commendations. He had never served in the military either. Without the extra points he had to study that much harder to get promoted, and study he did!

He came on the job a year after I did and was initially assigned to Manhattan, which is where I had met him for the first time. I'd never worked with him and I pride myself in not being the kind of cop who believes everything he hears. However, I can assure you that since becoming a Lieutenant, he never ventured past the front door of the PSA unless he had to. On those rare occasions he usually took, in addition to his driver, an extra cop.

"After all" he was fond of saying, "It's dangerous out there!"

I was about to walk back to the Administrative office when he said,

"Do me a favor and jot down on a piece of paper, the prisoner's name, address and a short story for the Blotter, just in case we get a visit from the Patrol Captain."

The "Blotter" was a rather large ledger book that is kept at the Desk into which the desk officers are required to make official entries. Entries such as the roll call for each tour, any arrests that are made, and by whom. Most importantly, the time a prisoner is brought into the PSA, and exactly when he left for Central Booking, is religiously recorded. Most bosses didn't like prisoners remaining in the PSA any more than necessary. You brought the prisoner in, did your paperwork, and out you went to Central Booking.

The longer it took you to get your ass downtown with the prisoner the more nervous the bosses would get, especially the likes of Lt. Romano. He was always worried that something would happen to the prisoner while he was in the PSA, something for which he would be held accountable.

Patrol Captains, with their unannounced visits, were capable of striking terror in the heart of individuals like Lt. Romano.

Romano was already agitated over the fact that almost an hour had gone by since the prisoner had come in, and he still didn't have enough information with which to put a "scratch" in the Blotter. The fact that he's a worrier is plainly visible in his beady little eyes that constantly darted about as if something horrible and unthinkable was about to happen.

Rumor had it that he, being small in stature, felt the need to take one of those "Dale Carnegie" courses on how to be more assertive. After finishing the course he went out and had a hair transplant in an attempt to cover his increasingly receding hairline.

Well, the transplant never really took and he lost quite a bit of his own hair in the process. Now he constantly wears a cap to cover his full head of non-growing hair plugs!

# Chapter 24

I WALKED INTO THE ADMIN office and found the rookie seated across from the prisoner who at the moment didn't appear too happy. I was relieved to see that he was still cuffed. The office is on the small side and being situated in the center of the station house, has no windows. There's only one door in and that is where I'm presently standing. I motion to O'Brien to join me outside the room for a moment, and once outside I ask him if the prisoner had made any statements.

"He hasn't said a word, other than wanting to go to the bathroom. I read him his rights again and he won't even tell me his name. I get the feeling that he's pissed off because I wouldn't let him use the bathroom." he added.

"Don't worry about it, his problems are only just beginning," I said.

We both step back into the room, and after removing his handcuffs, I ask him for his name and address. He's initially reluctant to give me that information, so I tell him that we don't really need to know what his name is because we'll just book him as John Doe. He'll be denied bail until he changes his mind and decides to cooperate. That seems to get his attention, so he tells me that his name is Justin Washington and lives at 360 Dumont Avenue. I jotted all this information on a small piece of paper. I add a list of tentative charges, and give it to the rookie to take out to Lt. Romano before he has a stroke. The charges, at least for now are, Criminal Trespass, and Attempted Rape.

# Chapter 25

**WELL LOOK WHO FINALLY** showed up, the cop they all been callin Cappy. Maybe we can get the ball rollin' now. Oh, oh, now what? He and Bill steps outside the office, and they start talkin' to each other real low. I can see, but I can't hear what they be sayin'. Now they both be back in the office, and the Cappy guy he tells me to stand up. As I gets to my feet he starts pattin' me down again. He finally takes off the cuffs and motions for me to head for a door that's not more than six feet from where I been sittin. He says that's the bathroom and that I can go in but I can't close the door. I finally get to take a leak and I make sure that I piss all over the toilet seat, hoping that the next cop to sit on it will pick up some kind of germs.

The older cop wants to know if I gots to take a shit and I tells him no, the urge has passed. I walk back out into the office not even botherin' to flush the toilet, and Cappy points to the chair and asks me to sit down.

I sense a change in his attitude and he actually seems to be goin' outta his way to be nice to me. He once again begins to explain to me what my rights are, only this time real slow. He's making sure that after each right is stated that I say "I understand" It's almost as if he wants to be my friend, or at least that's what he wants me to believe. What in the hell am I thinkin'?  This is a white cop sittin across from me, all this bullshit about rights, but I still aint seen a lawyer. All they keep sayin' is how I'm entitled to one be present, but aint nobody gone out and called one for me. This cop gives about as much a shit about me, as I do about him. I jest got to keep rememberin' that these bastards only want to put me away for as long as possible, and I'll be dammed if I'm gonna help em do it. I jest gotta stick to my story about only wantin' to help the kid. Shit, it's my word aginst hers, and I don't gotta prove nothing. I just hope they don't find that little plastic pill bottle that I shoved down between the seats in the back of the police car. I shoulda thrown that thing away, once I had her on the roof.

All I can say about this cop is, he sure gots a lot of patience. He jest keeps goin over and over the same shit. How long is it gonna take him to figure out that I'm not changin' my story. Shit, I'll play his silly little game, it's not hurtin me none. Will you jest listen to this shit, now he's tellin me that maybe I have a problem. Maybe I can't help what I do, and that I'll feel better if I jest get it off my chest.

Yeah, I got a problem, I want to tell em. I got caught, that's my problem. To think that I was almost beginnin' to like this guy, and now he's trying to tell me that I'm some kind of a weirdo. Well he can jest go to hell, cause now I'm really pissed off. Now he can kiss my black ass, before I tell him shit.

That little bitch wanted it as much as I did. She took my dollar didn't she? Hell, he can ask me questions till hell freezes over. I'm not tellin him nothin'!

Whatever I say is only gonna get turned around anyway, so I could look like the bad guy. I wonder if this cop has a kid, maybe a little girl. I wonder what he would say if I asked him? I better keep my mouth shut; he seems like the kind of asshole that would enjoy beatin' the shit outta me. I wish he would jest stop askin' all these bullshit questions, and maybe put me in a cell so I could get some sleep.

Now, he's tellin me to take off my clothes, what is he, some kinda nut? I try to tell em that I don't have nothing on me.

I get all undressed, jest like the man says. I've been through this before and I wondered if they wasn't kind of "getting off" by watching men naked. I shook out my socks to show that there was nothing hidden inside, When I asked him if he was finally satisfied, he tells me to turn around and bend over. The next thing I know he's tellin me to spread my cheeks. I hope he aint got no ideas about stickin' something up my butt. I straighten up and turn around to face him, and I see that he's lookin' down at my dick. He asks me why it looks like it had been bleedin', and I tell him that I got it caught in my zipper, you know, bein so big and all. The look he gives me says that he doesn't think that's so funny. It's really beginning to hurt, now that I'm thinkin about it. Maybe I ought to ask to go to the hospital. On second thought maybe I better not. He then tells me to get dressed, which I quickly do as it's startin' to get cold in here.

I had no sooner put my shoes back on, when in walks these two other white cops, both dressed in suits. This cop Cappy seems to know them on a first name basis. He calls the short stocky one Joe, and the other one Harry. I don't like the looks of these two guys. The one called Harry, smells like a brewery, and I'm sittin' at least eight feet away. He makes me nervous as he keeps lookin' over at me and smilin'. I get the feelin' that maybe he likes beatin' up on people and blacks in particular. He probably would like nothing better than to kick my ass all over this office. I could look at cops and almost read their minds.

# Chapter 26

**ONCE O'BRIEN HAD LEFT** the room I sat down facing the prisoner. I formerly introduced myself as Officer Caporusso and again very slowly, in a very deliberate manner, read him his rights. I'd seen veteran homicide detectives do it that way, and they seemed to always get the prisoner's cooperation. I also began forming certain opinions about Mr. Washington. He appeared outwardly calm, exhibiting very little anxiety. However, before removing his cuffs, I thoroughly patted him down for any weapons that I might have missed on my initial search. I always make it a point to place the palm of my hand against the chest of my prisoners. No matter how calm they try to act and may outwardly appear, they have very little control over their heart rate. Justin didn't disappoint me and re-enforced my theory. I had a problem counting his heart rate. It had to be well over 150 beats per minute, and I could almost hear it pounding away in his chest. He was scared and he might talk yet, that is if he didn't have a heart attack first. When I got to the part of the Miranda warnings where I ask, "Now that I have advised you of your rights, do you wish to make a statement", his reply was.

"Yes, I do!"

"Ok" I said, "let's hear your statement'"

"I was mindin' my own business, when I sees this little girl and she's cryin. So I ask her why she cryin, and she says some boys done beat her up, and I could see that she been hurt. She then asks me if I could help her find the boys that beat her up. I says, sure I could help her. She says they ran into the building and maybe they be hidein' on the roof So we goes up to the roof and we aint there but maybe a minute and you'all showed up, and arrested me for nothin."

I let him talk, implying from time to time that his was a very believable story. When he finally finished his account of what happened, I confronted him with what the girl had said. He became increasingly agitated and strongly denied doing anything to her. He again repeated that his only reason for being on that roof was to help her find the boys that had hurt her.

During his little speech, I noticed that from time to time, he would grab his groin and sort of pull at his trousers. He wasn't arrested for a drug violation, so we hadn't stripped searched him. It now dawned on me that he might indeed be a drug addict, and might very well have a set of "works" taped under his genitals. Junkies often do things like that, that's one of the reasons why we strip search them. A set of works had sometimes gone undetected until they got downtown, where they were automatically stripped searched before being placed in a cell. Seeing that I was getting absolutely nowhere with my line of questioning, I decided to give it a rest for a while. This might be a good time to strip search him and see exactly what was down in his groin that was bothering him so much.

I told him that we would check out everything that he had told us. However, before we could do that, we would have to thoroughly search him to make sure that he wasn't concealing any drugs. The fact that he didn't object to the search only made me even more suspicious about his behavior. This was one hell of a cool character.

He got to his feet as ordered, and while leaning against the desk, removed his shoes and socks. The stench was unbelievable, and I was seriously tempted to skip the rest of the search. He started to shake his socks out even before asked to do so, apparently he had been through the drill once or twice before. He took off his shirt and pants, which I carefully examined after having first removed his personal belongings and placing them on the desk. He had no wallet and only forty cents in change. I returned the change to him telling him to hold it I his hand. He remained standing there in his dingy jockey shorts which appeared to have a brownish stain on the front. I told him to remove he shorts. I then told him to turn around, bend over and spread his cheeks. He hesitated momentarily asking if this was really necessary, and when I said that it was, he complied.

I could plainly see that he wasn't concealing anything, so I told him to straighten up and turn around. It was after he had turned around that I noticed a small cut on the top of his penis. It had apparently bled a little and this is what had caused the brown stain on the front of his shorts. When I asked him how he had hurt himself, he quickly replied that he had caught his "thing" in his zipper. That was a good answer and under any other circumstances, I might have believed him but of course I wasn't buying it. I was now more anxious than ever to get hold of the ER doctor's report.

# Chapter 27

MY THOUGHTS WERE INTERRUPTED by the arrival of Detective Lieutenant Joe Durenno, and Detective Sergeant Harry Mulhern. I was sort of surprised when they both entered the office, as these two guys worked the Major Case Squad and normally didn't show up for sex crimes. I really hadn't asked anyone for any help with this one. Two years earlier while still a detective, I attended a week long seminar at Police Headquarters, dealing specifically with sex crimes.

At the conclusion of the seminar, my partner and I had been given certificates, designating us as "Sex Crimes Specialists". However, you don't tell a Detective Lieutenant to mind his own business, besides Joe and I were old friends. We had both been foot patrolman together, more years ago than even I care to remember.

I brought the both of them up to speed on what I had, and the story that the perp was maintaining. While the prisoner was putting his clothes back on, Joe suggested that maybe he and Harry should talk to him.

With that Harry handed me the keys to their car and Joe asked if I wouldn't mind running over to Dunkin Donuts, and picking up some coffee for all of us. As I was about to leave the office, having put my uniform jacket back on, Joe handed me a five dollar bill and told me to take my time getting back.

Now, what's goin on? They tellin the cop named, Cappy, to go gets coffee, and to bring back some donuts. Shit I'm gonna be left alone with these two bad looking dudes. "Beer breath" is still smilin', and is now tellin' me how the three of us is gonna have a heart to heart talk. While he's sayin' this he's takin off his jacket. He takes his gun, that looks to be the size of a small cannon out of its holster and hands it to the other cop.

I don't like the direction this shit is goin' in; I mean they know that they can't beat me, right? They can't force me to say nothin', even they know that. This is still America, aint it? Holy shit, the stocky one is locking the door, now that the other cop has left to go get the coffee. The one they called Harry just keeps smilin' as he gets closer to me. I'm out of my chair and backin' up to the wall. I decided that if he hits me, I'm goin down whether I need to or not. I picked up that little move in prison. When the hacks hit you, you made sure you went down, if you didn't go down, they would just keep hittin' you until you did. The idea was to keep em happy by lettin' em think that if they wanted to, they could really hurt you. I was just about to say somethin' when the big one pounds his ham sized fist into my stomach. The blow doubles me over, and with the wind knocked out of me; I starts to go down, the second blow caught me somewhere in the small of my back jest before I hit the floor. No need to fake it this time. The bastard was grinin' as he said, "So you like little girls!"

I knew that he wasn't finished with me yet, so I stayed down tryin' to cover my face as much as I could. This guy knew what he was doin' so none of the blows landed anywhere near my face, or anywhere else, where it might show.

The stocky one was taking what looked like a white electric cord from his jacket pocket, and began looking around the room for an outlet. The big one is lifting me off the floor and ordering me to strip. I notice that the electric cord is now plugged in, and the one they call Joe, is holding a bare ended wire in each hand. He's careful to keep the ends apart. I thinks to myself, these mothers are gonna "lectrocute me!"

This is getting a little too much for me, so I say to the big guy, "Maybe we could talk a little". He tells me one more time to strip, and I begin stammering,

"I didn't really mean to hurt the little girl. I jest didn't know what came over me"

The next thing I know is that I'm back in the chair; I'm cryin my head off and spillin' my guts to these two cops. The one called Joe has unplugged the electric cord and is putting it back in his pocket. A miniature tape recorder suddenly is on the desk, and in the next breath, I'm confessing to everythin'. I hate to think of where they were gonna attach those wires, if I hadn't decided to talk. All I want to do is get out of here in one piece.

On passing the Desk, on my way out, I noticed that O'Brien was engaged in a conversation with one of the other rookies.

Lt. Romano looked up from a book he was reading, and gave me a look, as if to say, "Where are you going?"

I told him that Lt. Durenno and Sgt. Mulhern were interviewing the prisoner, and that I had been sent out for coffee.

"I take cream and two sugars in mine, thank you", he quickly added.

# Chapter 28

**JOE DURENNO WAS JUST** hanging up the telephone when I walked into the office with the coffee and donuts. He had called the Brooklyn D.A.'s office to see if we could get the riding ADA to respond to the PSA. Apparently while I was gone, the prisoner had a change of heart and decided to make a full confession. Joe, although already having taped the prisoner's confession, felt that a video tape taken by the ADA would hold up better in Court. In addition to the fact that it's always better to get an ADA involved in a case as early as possible.

I am a bit curious as to why the prisoner had decided to make a confession, and I asked Joe. He dismissed the question with an off handed comment about him, the prisoner, "wanting to get it off his chest". I had a feeling that there was a lot more to it than just that, and I hoped that whatever it was , wouldn't come back to haunt me later.

Lt. Romano was making an entry in the Blotter to the effect that the prisoner, as per Lt. Durenno was still in the station house awaiting the arrival of the riding ADA. Knowing how nervous Romano gets, just being able to make that entry, and thereby justifying the prisoner's continued presence, probably helped bring his blood pressure back down to normal. I handed him a container of coffee, for which he thanked me. While turning away he mumbled something under his breath, something to the effect that, "everything is under control". I guess that was just his way of reassuring himself that he could no longer be held accountable for the delay in moving the prisoner downtown to Central Booking.

I still couldn't get over the change in the prisoner's demeanor. When I had left to get the coffee and donuts, he had been very adamant about his innocence. Now, since I'm back, he seems to have come completely unglued, and can't stop talking about his guilt, and how sorry he is for what happened. I wasn't sure as to whether I really wanted to know what had caused this "change of heart". He didn't look any the worse for wear, so they apparently hadn't beaten the confession out of him. However, he was visibly agitated, and kept looking over at Harry from time to time, who was quietly sipping his coffee and munching on a jelly donut.

In today's day and age, a case could be lost on a mere technicality, never mind, allegations of "Police Brutality" While the primary function of the police is to arrest the perpetrator, leaving the prosecution to the lawyers in the DA's office, the outcome of many a case depended heavily on how the police went about the job of gathering evidence.

While waiting for the ADA to arrive, I decided that now might be a good time to get together with the rookie, and bring our memo books up to date. I mentally re-constructed the sequence of events since our last memo book entry, which showed us entering 360 Dumont Avenue. I quickly entered the necessary details into my book, and once finished, handed it to the rookie, instructing him to copy the information exactly as I had written it. The fact that the entries needed to be exactly alike was very important as they formed the foundation on which a case sometimes rested. A year from now,  if and when the case finally came to trial, a sharp defense attorney would rip the prosecution's case to shreds by uncovering the smallest discrepancies between what the two of us had entered in our books.

Lt. Romano stepped into the office where O'Brien and I, were seated. He informed me that he had just received a call from the DA's office and that he'd been told that ADA Cathy Blassner was responding, and would probably be arriving shortly. I guess hearing the ADA's name startled me a bit, as Romano asked.

"Cappy, I guess you already know the broad?"

"Yeah, we met once before on another case." I quickly added, hoping to conceal my surprise.

# Chapter 29

**WHAT I'D TOLD ROMANO** wasn't necessarily the whole truth. Cathy Blassner and I had met about seven years ago. She was attending Law School at night, while holding down a Probation Officer's job during the day. I had arrested a fifteen year old for and Assault and Robbery on an eighty-two year old woman. Because of the juvenile's age, the case was to be adjudicated in Children's Court. The law has subsequently been changed so as to allow the Court, for certain "felonies", to prosecute such juvenile offenders as adults. However, back then if the case got past the Probation Department, the juvenile would be represented by a Law Guardian. The prosecution would be handled by the Corporation Counsel of the City of New York, instead of the DA's office.

It was Cathy's job as a Probation Officer to interview the juvenile and determine if the case could be resolved without having to resort to a hearing before a Family Court Judge. She made the determination as to whether the kid could benefit from counseling and thereby turn his life around. If the kid seemed beyond hope, the case would be placed on the Children's Court Calendar and heard by the Judge.

Cathy was very attractive, of medium height and weight, with blond hair and hazel eyes. She had the kind of figure that caused men to openly stare, and she knew it. Due to one of the cases I was working on at the time, she and I became good friends. I was to soon discover that it wasn't just my good looks and charm, but the fact that I was Italian that really turned her on. She had this thing about Italian men, and anything even remotely connected to Italy, like the Alfa Romeo that I drove. She had been born into a Jewish-Italian family, but was brought up in the Jewish faith. She secretly cherished her mother's Italian ancestry and longed to be a part of it.

I guess I had a lot going for me as far as she was concerned. Not only did I have the Italian looks, but I had also lived in Italy for a few years, having attended High School in Rome. I could also speak Italian, which she insisted that I do, whenever we were together. The fact that she understood very little of what I was saying, didn't faze her in the least. She loved the sound of the language and wanted to learn it from me.

It wasn't long before we were going to lunch together whenever I found myself down at "Kiddie Court". I also began arresting more juveniles, looking forward to those court appearances so as to be able to be with her more often.

Without ever intending to, I one day realized that I had fallen in love with her. Not a good thing when you're married with three children. She had never asked me if I were married, and I just assumed that she knew that I was. Several months after we met, she confided in me that she was going through divorce proceedings. She had been married a little over two years. She went on to explain that her husband was a very successful attorney, who had found it impossible to leave his work at the office.

In the beginning she hadn't minded so much, what with her beginning her evening studies at Brooklyn Law School. After a while, however, she began to feel that she was competing with his work for his attention at home. At first she was determined to make a go of the marriage, and had resigned herself to the fact that she would always come second to his work. When it became apparent that he was using his work to avoid her sexually, she decided to draw the line. She confronted him with her feelings, and asked if it were not true. Didn't he find her attractive, she'd asked? Had she done anything to make him feel inadequate? These were some of the questions that she posed to him.

All he could say was that he was sorry. Sorry for the whole mess and that he had sincerely thought that he could make it work but that he had been sadly mistaken.

She was everything that a man could want in a woman, but that was the crux of the problem. He was in love with someone else and that someone else happened to be a man. He hoped that she would someday forgive him, but would understand if she couldn't. From that day forward they slept in separate rooms, and it wasn't long before their marriage ended in Divorce Court.

She had apparently just gotten over the divorce when I entered her life. I loved her in a very special way, and had I not been married with children, something would have surely come out of our friendship. However, my wife was my wife, and I took my marriage vows very seriously. To continue the relationship wouldn't be fair to Cathy, nor to my wife. Cathy needed to get on with her life.

Due to one reason or another, we began to see less and less of each other in the ensuing weeks. I'd heard that she had eventually left the Probation Department, and we never ran into each other again.

# Chapter 30

**ADA CATHY BLASSNER** was, in addition to being an extremely competent criminal attorney, also a very attractive woman. The Kings County DA's office, with their less than competitive wages, were indeed fortunate in having her on their staff, She had graduated second in her class at Brooklyn Law, and had been offered, even before passing the Bar Exam, excellent positions from several prestigious law firms. However, having worked as a Probation Officer for several years before finishing law school, she felt that she would be more comfortable on the prosecution side of the fence, rather than the defense. Make no mistake about it, the higher salaries offered by the private firms, were certainly tempting but she had turned them down. She hoped that with the eventual advancement in the DA's office, would also come the advances in pay. At least that was how it had been explained to her when she agreed to accept her present position.

She had started out like the rest of the new grads, in the Arraignment Part of the Criminal Court, where arrested individuals are brought before a Judge for the first time. It's there that they are initially charged with a specific crime. After hearing the facts set forth in the complaint, bail is usually set by the presiding Judge, and a return date is agreed upon by both the DA's office and the defense attorney.

It is between the arraignment and the return date that the cases are prepared for a Preliminary Hearing.

During this hearing another Judge will hear the facts of the case, and applicable arguments from both sides. Based on this hearing, the Judge will decide whether the State has a "Prima Facie" case against the defendant.

If the Judge concludes that the State does indeed have a case, the defendant will be ordered to stand trial. A mutually agreeable date will be picked for the commencement of the trial.

In Felony cases like Murder, Rape, Robbery, Arson, and Burglary, a Grand Jury will usually hear testimony and make a determination as to whether to indict the defendant, and order a trial.

However, the decision as to whether items of evidence are admissible is always left to the Judge and his expertise of the Law.

Some overzealous Legal Aid attorneys, instead of just confining their argument at the arraignment to the question of bail, and whether or not their client can be expected to return to Court on the date specified, actually attempt to "try" the case right then and there!

This action on their part actually slows down the whole process. Unfortunately for their client, this sometimes irritates the Judge, who is usually overwhelmed by the large number of cases that he is expected to rule on in one day. If he has to continually remind the attorneys that this is primarily a bail proceeding, and not a trial, someone in all likelihood will be on the receiving end of his frustration. If you guessed that that someone was the defendant, you were absolutely right!

There have been instances where defendants, based on the circumstances of the crime, should have been released in their own recognizance, but were remanded with high bail in large measure because of the antics of their attorney.

Cathy had learned early in her career that it just didn't pay to antagonize a sitting Judge, with superfluous arguments. They, for the most part usually went along with the recommendation of the District Attorney's office. In the few instances where they didn't, arbitrarily setting a low bail or no bail at all, there really was nothing to be gained by arguing the point, as Judges were not inclined to change their minds.

After spending over a year in arraignments, she was moved up the ladder to trial preparation, where she was quickly getting the reputation of a tough adversary.

Cathy had only been home a little over an hour, having stopped downtown to do some shopping after leaving the office. Having just stepped out of the shower, she was in her bedroom standing naked before her full length mirror admiring her well-proportioned figure. She was especially proud of her breasts, and the fact that they hadn't yet begun to sag. That was something that quite often occurred when your bra size was a 40 D.

As she toweled herself dry, she heard the telephone ringing in the living room. Not bothering to put on a robe she went to answer it, thinking that it was probably Stefano. They had planned to have dinner together. She was a little disappointed when after answering she recognized the voice of Officer Timothy Fox.

"Ms. Blassner?" He inquired, with a hint of sarcasm in his voice. Fox was assigned to the DA's office, not so much for his ability as a Police Officer, but more as a sort of answering service for the ADAs who were "On Call".

Right from the very first time that they'd met, she had developed a strong dislike for him. He always managed to come up with off-color comments that he thought were cute. These remarks usually had some sort of sexual connotation, and were often followed by disgusting gestures that he rarely attempted to conceal.

"This is Cathy Blassner" she answered, not at all trying to mask the contempt in her voice.

"Ms. Blassner", he continued, over emphasizing the Ms. "This is Fox down at the office. I hope I haven't disturbed you. I just received a call from a Lieutenant Durenno over in

Housing's PSA 2. It seems that your beautiful body is desperately needed there"

Cathy, unable to control her anger, replied. "Listen asshole, just cut the shit and explain to me exactly what it is that you are trying to say, Ok?"

"Whoa, aren't we touchy this evening, I guess I must have really interrupted something big!"

"Listen Fox", continued Cathy, realizing that dealing with this idiot was a no win situation.

"Just give me the information you were asked to relay, and cut the stupid shit. I'm in no mood for your juvenile games."

This was not the first time that he had succeeded in pissing her off. When she had complained to her boss, Ira Greenberg, Ira just shrugged his shoulders and tapped the side of his head with his index finger. Fox's' behavior was known by everyone in the office and most of the attorneys had come to the conclusion that he wasn't dealing with a full deck. His gun had been taken away from him after a Police Department psychiatrist had concluded that he was not only a danger to himself, but more importantly a danger to the public as well. He was being allowed to bide his time while waiting for the Department's Medical Review Board to decide on his Pension.

Actually, Fox was one of the many Police Officers jokingly assigned to the rubber gun squad. They were the cops who were taken off the street, hidden in an office somewhere, and ultimately pensioned off with some sort of psychological disability.

Apparently recognizing that he had pissed her off enough for one evening, he continued.

"Like I said, some Lieutenant over in PSA 2 called, and said that one of their guys locked up some creep for sexually assaulting a kid on the roof of one of the projects buildings. They need you to take a confession from the perp, and also a statement from the kid. Did I make myself clear enough, counselor?"

"Consider the message received. When can I expect a driver to pick me up, or hadn't you thought of that yet?

"I think of everything babe, driver, photographer, everything! He should be ringing your doorbell any minute now. How's that for service, sweetheart! Ha-ha".

Cathy slammed down the phone to the sound of the asshole laughing on the other end. Exactly why they had to assign him to the DA's office was beyond her. They could have just as easily put him in charge of counting the wooden barricades. It was rumored that he was related to a political big shot in the Mayor's office, someone that no one dared to offend.

What bothered her, even more than his lewd remarks, was the bullshit on the telephone, and how you almost had to literally kiss his ass to get the information. His only duty from four to midnight, Monday thru Friday, was to answer the telephone and relay messages to the riding ADA. He had the Duty Roster and their home telephone numbers, which also concerned her a bit, as she had on a number of occasions been awakened during the night by the phone ringing only to hear heavy breathing on the other end. She would not for one minute put it past him to pull a stunt like that.

If he couldn't reach the ADA at home, he would contact them by calling their beeper numbers. That was all that was expected of him. He probably felt that even that was asking too much of him. Depending on who was on call, and whether he liked the person or not, he would sometimes try to talk the callers into calling back in the morning insisting that their problem wasn't important enough to bother an ADA. People had complained about this also, and he had been instructed that it wasn't his job to screen calls. He was just to pass along the information to whoever was on call. Those instructions, no matter how many times they were given to him always seemed to fall on deaf ears.

Cathy was convinced that he derived a deviant pleasure out of the fact that he was ruining whatever plans the On Call ADA may have made for the evening. Such was certainly the case with Cathy tonight.

"That son of a bitch", she thought to herself, "One of these days, I'm going to nail his ass to the wall!"

She went back into her bedroom and was just pulling on a pair of panties, when she heard the doorbell ring. She shouted, "I'll be right there", and threw on her terry cloth bathrobe before going to answer the door. To her surprise it wasn't the driver, but Stefano. He being early saved her the trouble of having to call him and cancel their date. As he entered the apartment, she said.

"Stefano darling, I was just about to call you and beg off for tonight. I have to go over to Brownsville and take some statements, and I really don't know how long I'm going to be. Why don't we make it tomorrow night?"

*"Cara mia"*, moaned Stefano with an exaggerated frown, as he playfully tugged at the terrycloth belt that held Cathy's robe closed. Without warning the belt came undone and the front of the robe parted. Cathy, although embarrassed, made no attempt to close the robe and thereby cover her exposed breasts.

Stefano, not one to pass up an opportunity, quickly buried his face between the two warm and soft mounds of flesh. Cathy began softly stroking the back of his head while whispering words of encouragement. He took the hint, and began to eagerly suck on the now erect pale pink nipple of her right breast, as she continued to caress his head.

Coming up for air, Stefano began smothering Cathy with kisses causing her to almost loose her breath. She was beginning to feel a stirring from within the front of his trousers, that only a moment before had not existed. Realizing that it would be pointless to try to put him off, and really not wanting to either, she suggested a quickie, as he so aptly sometimes called them.

She had begun to help him remove his trousers when again the doorbell sounded. Cathy got up off her bed, where they had finally wound up, and began pulling her panties back on for what seemed like the second time in less than an hour.

"Sweetheart, you have to get dressed", she told Stefano. "That's my driver, who is here to drive me to Brownsville."

Seeing that Stefano hadn't moved so much as an inch, she continued, "Honestly, 'amore mio', I really have to leave! We can continue this later tonight, I promise!" She had to turn away quickly to avoid the look on his face, which at any

108

moment, might start her laughing. She again went to the front door, asking, "Who's there?"

Recognizing the voice of her driver, she was just about to open the door, when looking down, she noticed that she hadn't yet put on a bra, and was standing there in only her panties. She shouted for him to wait a second, and ran back to the bedroom where Stefano was standing there with her bra in his hand.

"I thought you might need this", he said. She quickly got into her bra and he helped her with the hooks in back. She grabbed her blouse from a nearby chair, and while buttoning it up, located her shoes under the bed. She slid into her skirt, the same one that she had worn all day, and stepped into her shoes in what looked like a much practiced maneuver. She then gave a petulant Stefano a quick kiss, and brazenly rubbed her hand against the area of his trouser that still bulged a bit.

"Later, 'tesoro mio', she whispered. As she again went to the front door, only this time she was fully dressed.

She had been seeing Stefano, off and on for the past two years. The relationship, over the last three months, had taken on a much more intimate nature. In fact, he had already proposed to her, but she kept putting off the thought of marriage, not yet being ready to again make such a commitment. She had told Stefano all about her short lived marriage, and how it had ended. She felt that if he truly loved her as much as he claimed he did, he would wait until she was ready. They seemed to be well matched in every respect. He was thirty four and a successful dentist, with his own practice. He had also been married for a short period of time, but his wife, also a dentist, had some pretty powerful connections in the Catholic Church and instead of a divorce, she managed to get the marriage annulled.

He was now, Cathy's Italian stallion, as his good looks and athletic physique, as well as his prowess in the bedroom often prompted her to say.

There was however, a dark side to his personality that she hadn't yet been able to figure out. Not too often, but every once in a while he would seem to withdraw into himself locking her out, along with everything else.

She has a hunch that it had something to do with his prior marriage. Other than the fact that his former wife had been a year older than him, and they had both attended the same dental college in Pennsylvania, she knew very little about his past.

She really hoped that she wouldn't be tied up all night, as she already missed Stefano, and the promise of what was to come later that evening.

The ride from her apartment on Clark Street in Brooklyn Heights to the PSA in Brownsville, took a lot longer than she had expected. Her driver, nearing sixty-five and retirement, had refused to take the local streets saying that driving along Atlantic Avenue was much too dangerous. He insisted on taking the long way around via the Belt Parkway. That meant that they would be driving all the way around the bottom of Brooklyn and past Coney Island. This added an additional thirty minutes to the trip. Plus they would have to contend with the Long Island bound commuters on the Belt Parkway.

They finally reached the PSA and she helped carry in some of the video equipment. At this point she'd do anything that would help speed things up, and thereby get her back to her apartment that much sooner where Stefano had promised to wait.

She introduced herself to a somewhat disheveled looking Lieutenant standing behind the Desk. This guy was one for the books; he actually asked to see her ID. She came close to asking him how many times in the past had a young white woman entered his station house and tried to pass herself off as an ADA. What an asshole! After taking his sweet time recording all her information in his Blotter, he directed her to the Admin Office where he said the arresting officer was waiting with the prisoner.

Upon entering the office, she noticed a black prisoner handcuffed to a nearby handhold, which was bolted to the wall. He must be the child molester. Standing to the right of the prisoner with their backs facing the door she had just entered, stood two uniformed cops both making entries in their memo books.

She cleared her throat in an attempt to get their attention and when they turned she saw that one of them looked very familiar. A little older perhaps, but apparently none the worse for wear. A forgotten part of her past had just caught up with her as Officer Caporusso smiled and extended his had to shake hers.

# Chapter 31

"Caporusso" I said, answering the telephone on the second ring.

"Cappy, this is Roberts, and I'm still at the hospital with the kid and her mother, I thought you might be interested in the Preliminary Report."

"What'd they find?" I asked.

"Well for openers, the kid was raped, there's no doubt about that. There was penetration. The bastard tore the shit out of her down there, and they found semen all over the place."

"Do me a favor. Make sure you get something in writing before you leave the hospital. I don't care if it's only a couple of lines on a piece of paper. Just make sure the emergency room doc signs it. The official report will probably take a couple of weeks. I don't want this guy walkin' on us and to keep that from happening, I'm gonna need that piece of paper when I testify at the hearing.

"I'll try, but you know how some of these doctors are, especially the foreign ones, they don't like to put their names to anything. By the way, that scumbag must have wiped his dick with the kid's underwear. One of the nurses told me that they found areas where semen was mixed in with blood."

The lousy bastard, I thought to myself.

"How's the kid's mother holding up through all of this?" I asked.

"Not all that bad. I mean if this had been my kid, I'd be foaming at the mouth by now. She's just sitting in the waiting room talking to some guy who just walked in."

"Ok, Roberts, stay close to them and bring em both back to the PSA when they finish treating the kid. We've got an ADA coming in who is probably gonna want to take a statement from both the kid and the mother." I said.

"No problem, catch you later."

"Take care", I said and hung up the phone.

"That was Robert's calling from the hospital, in case you missed it." I said to the rookie. I also noticed that the prisoner was all ears, and probably hadn't missed a word of what I had said while talking with Roberts.

I walked over to the rookie and lowering my voice, quickly brought him up to speed on what Roberts had told me.

A few moments later, hearing someone enter the room I turned around and saw Cathy Blassner standing just inside the doorway with her mouth agape.

She hadn't changed at all and the years had been good to her. Regaining my composure and not sure what else to do, I extended my hand somewhat formally while saying,

"Cathy, it's good to see you again!" She appeared to hesitate a moment, possibly unsure as to why I was being so formal after how close we had been. She then extended her hand as if to shake my hand, but instead wrapped her arms around me and gave me one hell of a friendly hug. I was taken aback a little by her open display of affection and I couldn't help but savor the moment before disengaging myself. I took one step back and said,

"You look absolutely great!"

"Thanks, that's nice of you to say, and hadn't you have said it, I would have "popped" you one right in the old schnazolla, she said laughing. "So what's with the uniform, been a bad boy lately?"

"You would think so, wouldn't you? I'll tell you all about it later. Let's get this guy's statement, before he changes his mind." I said.

Cathy reached for my hand again and gave it a quick squeeze, and said.

"It's really great seeing you again; we've got a lot to catch up on." Letting go of my hand, she was once again, all business.

She quickly told us how she wanted the chairs placed and what wall she would use for the backdrop, on which the wall clock would be hung. The use of the wall clock with its' constantly moving second hand, kept a defense attorney from alleging that the video tape had been altered or tampered with.

Once everything was in place, Cathy asked me to remove the prisoner's handcuff that had been attached to bar along the wall. She then asked me to sit the prisoner in the chair that had been placed slightly off to the right of the clock. The clock had been plugged in and the correct time had been set. I watched as she took the chair on the other side of the table, directly across from where the prisoner now sat. They seemed to both stare at each other for several seconds, and then he bent his head forward and looked down at the top of the table.

"Mr. Washington, My name is Catherine Blassner and I'm the Assistant District Attorney who has been assigned to this case. I've been told by Officer Caporusso, that you would like to make a statement about what occurred on the roof where you were arrested. But before you make any statements or answer any questions, I want to advise you of your Constitutional Rights. If after I advise you of your Rights you still choose to make a statement, I'll be happy to take that statement. I'm now going to turn on the video camera and we will begin."

She turned to her driver, who also doubled as camera operator and told him to begin filming. Cathy began to slowly read the prisoner his Miranda Warnings. Once that was completed she said,

"Mr. Washington, would you please state your name, your date of birth, and your address, for the purpose of this videotaped confession. If at any time during this interview you decide that you want to stop, you only need to say so. Would you please begin."

The interview took forty-three minutes; during which time he said that "yes" he tried to have sex with the little girl, after making her perform oral sex. All of this happened after he got her to the roof, after asking her to help him find a sick lady. He said he only hit her once or twice, when she tried to run away. The most outrageous part of the statement was when he said,

"I swear I didn't know she was twelve years old, until the police told me. I thought she was only six or seven."

After the interview was over and the prisoner had been temporarily placed in one of the empty holding cells, Cathy said to me,

"I don't know how in the world any defense attorney is going to be able to mount a defense after the jury hears that confession."

"Stranger things have happened, you just never know." I said.

With the completion of his confession, her part of the job was done.

Moments later I walked to the Desk to advise Lt. Romano that the interview had been completed and that the prisoner would soon be leaving for Central Booking. A Sergeant was filling in for him, as he was taking a personal break. I went back to the Admin Office where Cathy and her driver were packing up there equipment.

"Has the little girl come back from the hospital?' Cathy asked.

"Not yet they haven't completed their examination. I can tell you", I said, "That the preliminary report that I got from one of the officers over the phone confirms the Rape at this time. They even found some of his semen on the kid's underwear."

"That son of a bitch had the nerve to say that he thought she was six or seven and not twelve. I felt like jumping across the desk and choking the shit out of him myself." She said.

"Who knows, maybe that'll be his defense. 'I'm just a sick soul, who couldn't help myself', that might just get him off'. I said.

"Not if I have anything to do with it. They should bring back "Capital Punishment" for bastards like him." she said.

"I wouldn't hold my breath if I were you" I said, adding, "By the way, I notified the Sex Crimes Unit, and they'll have someone at Court in the AM to talk to the kid and her mother.

"I see you haven't lost your touch, you still think of everything." She said.

"Not nearly everything, I'm afraid" I said, while gesturing to the fact that I was wearing a uniform.

"That's right you were going to tell me about that."

"That story will take a lot more time than we have right now. Maybe I could give you a call, and we could get together over a drink or something?"

"I'd love to." She said, as she jotted down her home number on one of her business cards.

"Call me anytime, just don't wait too long!"

Feeling as if her last statement had been a green light, I felt that it was now my turn to embrace her and I did, while whispering in her ear, "I've missed you, I really have, especially our time together."

As I let go of her, she stepped back and said, "Me too.", and with that she turned to leave. On her way out the door she turned to look back at me, and waved saying, *"Ciao caro!"*

I guess she still hasn't gotten over Italians, I thought to myself and with that I returned to the problems at hand.

Under any other circumstances I would have cuffed the prisoner's hands behind his back, placed in the front seat of my private vehicle, fastened his seat belt and drove him down to Central Booking. Once you strap a handcuffed prisoner into the front seat, it would take the talent of Harry Houdini for him to free himself. I decided that this was a collar that I just wasn't going to take any chances with. All that had to happen was for some drunk to broadside my car on the way downtown. I'd probably spend what little time I had left on the job trying to justify to his attorney's just why I had transported him in my private vehicle.

I asked Lt. Romano to call in one of the RMPs and ten minutes later the prisoner and I were on our way to Central Booking, which is located on the second floor of the eight-four Precinct.

The trip downtown didn't take very long and it was around 9:00 p.m. when we pulled into the rear parking area. The officer who had driven us downtown stepped out of the car and opened the rear door for us, while the other officer said.

"Do you want me to walk you upstairs?"

"I'll be ok, thanks anyway", which I said while taking a firm grip of the prisoner's arm and steering him in the direction of the back door to the building. The stairway leading upstairs was always well lit and about eight feet wide. I had no problem with the prisoner whose hands were still cuffed behind his back. I pushed the button that was located just to the side of the locked door and turned slightly to my left so my image could be picked up by the closed circuit TV camera. There was the immediate sound of a buzzer which unlocked the door and allowed us to enter.

"Hey, Cappy", said the officer behind the long counter on my left. "What have you got for us tonight?"

"Well, for openers," I said, "Rape, Sodomy, and a few other things, that I'll be adding on down the road."

"Sounds like you've had a busy little evening, my man." said the BCB officer to the prisoner. "You're lucky that it was Cappy here who busted you and not me. I aint got no use for preverts! Stand with your back against the wall and face the camera."

With that the prisoner was photographed with a Polaroid camera. Another officer handed me a large packet of forms that had to be filled out for the booking process. I took my handcuffs off the prisoner and handed him over to another officer who would do a strip search, and fingerprint him.

"Are you gonna need this guy after I print him?" asked the officer who was leading my prisoner away.

"Not really, I've got everything I'm gonna need in the way of information. You can put him into one of the holding cells when you're done with him." I said.

There were some detectives from other commands that I was friendly with, and they kept up a steady barrage of comments about how "good" I looked in my "new uniform."

Central Booking is almost like a social club. You usually ran into the same faces, the cops that worked hard at keeping the streets of the City a little safer by locking up the bad guys, and also racking up a lot of overtime money in the process. They used to refer to it as "collars for dollars."

Every once in a while you'd see a lost soul with his first arrest, trying to figure out what he had to do next. Sometimes a new face meant someone who was ordered to make an arrest. More than likely, a collar that no one else would touch with a ten foot pole. Either because it wasn't worth the effort, or because the prisoner had sustained some injuries when he "resisted arrest!"

I didn't want to waste too much time socializing with the guys tonight, as I had received word that my complainant and her mother were waiting for me over on the DA's side of the building. I found an empty chair at one of the long desks around which, on one side sat the police officers, and on the other side sat the prisoners with one hand free to sign papers, and the other handcuffed to metal pipes securely attached to the wall.

I was halfway through my paperwork, when all of a sudden; there was a huge commotion on my left. A prisoner being escorted into the holding area apparently decided that he didn't like the idea of being handcuffed to the metal pipe and at that moment was scuffling with his arresting officer. I jumped out of my chair intending to help subdue the unruly prisoner. Before I could get no more than a couple of feet there were six very big cops from the BCB staff all over the prisoner. He had gotten in a lucky punch, as I could see some blood trickling from the officer's nose. At this point the sight of the officer's bloody nose was not lost on the cops from BCB. They now had the prisoner immobilized and he was being led away to a large room to the right of the holding area. There had to be at least ten officers and probably twelve to fifteen prisoners all talking away moments before the incident. Now you could hear a pin drop, that's how quiet it had gotten. A moment later, the door to the room that the unruly prisoner had been taken to was heard slamming shut. In the next instant the silence was shattered by the blood curdling screams of the guy that had just been escorted into that other room. The screaming went on nonstop for four of five minutes and then it quieted down. The six BCB cops exited the room and I noticed that some were breathing a little heavier than others; they'd apparently gotten a little out of shape! The other thing that I noticed was that all six were smiling. It had an effect on the other prisoners that were being processed. I had never, in all my days at BCB seen a more respectful group of prisoners.

# Chapter 32

**YOU KNOW HOW THEY TELL YOU** that you are entitled to one free phone call when you been arrested; well you can take it from me, that's a crock a shit! What they don't tell you is yeah, you get to make the call, but only when they wants you to make the call. Plus you don't gets no privacy talkin, either!

I was finally finished bein' fingerprinted by some big bastard who looked like he was jest hopin' that I'd give him an excuse, anything at all, to beat the shit outta me. I gots up the nerve to politely ask if I could call my wife to let her know where I was. He told me that my arrestin' officer was the one that I had to ask, not him.

I was then handcuffed to some iron handrail and told to sit my ass down. After a little while the dude that arrested me comes over to where I'm sittin, and parks his ass on the chair across from me.

"Hey officer", I says. "When can I make my phone call that I'm supposed to be able to make?"

"You wanna make a phone call?" he says to me. "Shit, why didn't you say so? What's the number; I'll dial it for you?"

"Man, I can dial it myself, thank you!"

"Man, that aint the way it works! I dial the number and you get to talk, unless of course, you really don't want that call after all."

My momma didn't raise me, but still I was no fool. I gots the message so I gives him the number to call Darlene. He writes it down on one of them forms he been fillin' out, and then dials the number on one of the phones sittin on top of the long table. After he finished dialin' the number I reached with my free hand for him to give me the phone, but he don't hands it to me. When it sounded like it was answered he asks whoever it was that answered, what their name be and I could see he be writin' Darlene on the paper with the number already on it. Without so much as a look in my directions, he starts tellin Darlene that he be the police and that he arrested her husband for the rape of a little girl and only then do he hand me the phone.

"Hello, Darlene?" I says.

"You no good rotten motha fucker! I hope you rots in jail! Don't you be callin here no more! You hear what I'm sayin, you motha fucker!"

The next thing I hears, before I could even get a word in was the sound of the dial tone. The bitch had hung up on me. I handed the phone back to the cop not knowin' what to say.

"She hang up on you?" he asks.

"Yeah, she hung up, alright." I says.

"Don't feel so bad. Shit like that happens all the time." He says, and then laughs.

I think to myself, "What was that last comment supposed to do, make me feel better or something?"

I sat there thinkin about how long it would take these police to come up with the shit about my other arrests. I was worried; in particular about the time I got busted accused of killin' Karen, my daughter. Even though I managed to beat that one, it was thrown outta Court after Darlene changed her testimony. Would they look back and try to connect that case with this one? I couldn't trust Darlene no more. She, sure as shit would try to mess me up big time on this one.

It wasn't like I really wanted to kill my daughter; after all she was my own flesh and blood. Somethin' jest snapped somewhere in my head that day, and I guess I jest lost it. By the time I had finally come around to thinkin' straight, it was already too late. I mean didn't I go to the hospital with the kid? Trouble was she was already hurt too bad to do anythin', and in less than twenty-four hours, she was dead.

The hospital people said that someone had beat her real bad, and sure as shit, Darlene pointed to me.

The nurses had already called the police and I was arrested right there and then. One minute I'm talkin to the doctors and the next minute, the cops are cuffin me, and putting me in the back seat of a police car. I guess the Court assigned me a legal aid lawyer and when we finally get to talk, he tells me that I'm being charged with Manslaughter. My bail was higher than even I know how to count, cause Darlene told em that if I got out, I'd take off down South.

Naturally the bitch puts all the blame on my ass, sayin' that I flew into a rage over the kid drinkin' the last of the Kool-Aid. Shit, that wasn't the whole reason but talkin about it aint gonna do me no good.

I sat in a cell up on Rikers for almost a whole year, before the day of the trial finally come. I had got up tight with some brothers up on the rock who managed to get word out through their friends tellin Darlene that she better come and visit me. She started comin to visit after a couple of months and I guess I got through to her how she had better have a change of heart when it comes time to testify. I was able to convince her that I had really changed, that I loved her and I didn't mean for the kid to die like that. Getting me sent to prison wasn't gonna bring Karen back, and who could she get to take care of her, if I went to prison.

In the end she finally agreed to change her story when she was put on the stand during the trial. She had to make it sound convincing to the Judge and Jury, and she did.

She testified that she had to clear her conscious. Her husband hadn't been the one to beat her daughter. It was a couple of Puerto Ricans that she had surprised breakin into her apartment when she had come home from shopping. That's when her daughter had tried to run from the apartment, and one of those guys had beaten her. She said that the reason she had blamed her husband, was because she had caught him having an affair with another woman, and she figured this would be a good way to get back at him. She knew that those Puerto Ricans would never be caught so she blamed Justin, never once thinkin' how much trouble he would really be facin'. She said that she was too scared, up until now, to come forward and tell the truth.

It worked like a charm, although I don't think that the ADA really believed her, but there really wasn't too much that they could do, as the Judge declared a mistrial and the charges against me were dropped. The DA's office charged Darlene with Perjury for her original statement but those charges went nowhere and were quickly forgotten.

Things between me and Darlene had gotten a little better for a while, but it wasn't long before we were fightin' again. She kept expectin' me to get a job and I didn't think I needed a job. We was both getting checks from the City every two weeks and if we needed a little extra cash, I could always take her over to Manhattan and pimp her ass off to some out of towners, that we could then rob for their money.

SOME CALL IT JUSTICE

# Chapter 33

IT WAS SEVERAL DAYS LATER on a Wednesday that I received a Notification, ordering me to appear before the Grand Jury the following morning at 9:30 a.m. It was further ordered that I bring all written reports and evidence in the case of the People of the State of New York vs. Justin Washington. I recall the ADA from the Sex Crimes Unit saying that he was going to present to a Grand Jury as quickly as he could, but I didn't think that it would be this soon. My scheduled 4 X 12 tour for Thursday would be automatically changed to a 9 to 5, however, I was still due in later this afternoon for my 4 X 12 tour. I hated Court Appearances after a 4 X 12. I lived out on Long Island in Suffolk County. That meant that I didn't normally arrive home until after 1 o'clock in the morning. I had to be up no later than 5:30 for the commute back to the City in order to be in Court by 9 or 9:30. If you wound up spending the entire day in Court, which was usually the case, your ass would be dragging on the drive back home later that afternoon. In order to eliminate this hassle I would sometimes sleep at my mother-in-laws the night before. She still lived in Brooklyn not too far from the Court House, downtown. In the morning I could sleep until 8, and still make it to Court by 9:00. I called my mother-in-law's house to let one the kids know that I would be sleeping over. They knew that I would probably show up after mid-night and wouldn't lock the outside door at 11:00 p.m., as was their custom. My wife's mother owned a six family house, with three of the apartments occupied by the immediate family. I usually slept on the second floor in one of the bunk beds. My mother-in–law, God bless her, had eight children, two boys and six girls. Three of the eight children are married and out of the house, so I always had a place to sleep on the nights that I needed to stay in the City.

The next morning I was forced to park two blacks from the Supreme Court on Adams Street and it was 9:15 by the time I signed in. I had to hunt around to find out exactly which Grand Jury was handling my case. In the City of New York, contrary to popular belief there are as many as four or five Grand Juries sitting at one time in each of the five boroughs. Richmond may have less due to its size. My case hadn't made the Calendar that had been printed up a week earlier. The case would be an "add-on" and it took me about twenty minutes to track down the ADA scheduled to present the case. I was happy to see that the rookie was there, but no sign of the complainant yet. I walked out to the front lobby thinking that maybe she and her mother might be out there. On the way back to the Grand Jury area I asked one of the uniformed officers in the corridor assigned to the Court to keep an eye open for a small black girl and her mother. The rookie was still assigned to the academy, but had been ordered to report to the Brooklyn Supreme Court for a Grand Jury appearance. While O'Brien was dressed in uniform, I had brought in my suit the previous day. We exchanged some small talk and apparently he had become somewhat of a celebrity in his class as a result of the arrest we had made. He said some of the other rookies hadn't believed him when he told them about the collar. But all doubt was dispelled when he got the notification to appear today. A couple of minutes later, the kid and her mother showed up and I breathed a sigh of relief. They were accompanied by another individual that I was to later discover was yet another "friend" of the family. The ADA assigned to the case had called in sick and a recently hired law school graduate was filling in for him. We must have gone over the details of the arrest a dozen times before he finally got it straight and even then I was a little worried that he'd screw it up.

You really have to try very hard to mess up a case in front of a Grand Jury. The members of the Jury are your captive audience, as the ADA presenting the case you have no competition since the defendant's attorney in not present and therefore can't object to anything that you say. What you have is a group of people to whom you tell a story. The story paints the picture of the crime. You support your story with the testimony of various witnesses, police officers, and your victim. You then go on to explain that there can be no doubt what-so-ever that the person that the police arrested committed the crime. With all that accomplished the Jury then votes on whether or not to indict the arrested individual for the crime. Very few people aren't indicted, that's just the way the system works. Whether that person is convicted at trial, well that's another matter. What the Grand Jury in their Indictment is saying is that, "Yes, there seems to be sufficient evidence to indicate that the person arrested did commit the crime." The defendant, on the advice of his attorney can testify but unless they are granted immunity, which is out of the question, they'd be a fool to appear and testify. It is not in their best interests as it is the State's job to prove that they committed the crime and not the other way around.

We were again told to have a seat in the waiting room, that our case would be called as soon as he could fit it in. When noon rolled around and we still hadn't been called I was starting to get a little pissed. I went looking for my little nervous ADA and managed to catch him just as he was about to leave the building for lunch. When I asked him why he was leaving for lunch without even having the decency to let us know, he became indignant, stating that he had asked one of the other ADAs to tell us. He went on for about a minute or two about how he really wasn't even supposed to be on this case, that someone in the Indictment Bureau had asked him to take the case for him and that he had his own caseload to worry about, let alone this other "shit" that had been dumped on him.

I don't know what came over me, for the next thing I knew I was grabbing this low life by his jacket and slamming him against the marble wall of the lobby. My right arm came back and I was about to plant my fist in his ugly pimply face, when all of a sudden my arms were pinned behind my back by two of the biggest Court Officers I had ever seen. They must have been standing close by when they saw the commotion. The little scumbag was now shouting about how I had threatened him. I had to talk pretty fast, as the two Court officers looked as if they were considering doing a number on me. Luck was on my side, as the head of the Indictment Bureau was himself heading out to lunch. He walked over and told the officers to release me. Al was a personal friend of mine; we had worked many a case together when he was an ADA assigned to the Criminal Court. I tried explaining to Al how this ADA and I had a difference of opinion over the handling of a particular case. The ADA had composed himself by now and seeing that his boss and I were on a first name basis thought better of insisting that I had threatened him. After dismissing the two officers, Al took the two of us back to his office. Once we were safely behind closed doors, with instructions to his secretary that he was not to be disturbed, he asked what the hell was going on. I told him exactly what had transpired between us from the very first moment that we met that morning in Court, ending with his comments about, "my shit case."

Al then gave the ADA a chance to tell his side of the story which made very little sense at all. The little creep was apparently on the verge of a nervous breakdown and Al sensing that, told him to take the rest of the day off and report directly to him in the morning.

After the guy had left, Al made a point of reminding me how lucky I had been that he happened along when he did. No matter how off base the asshole ADA had been, I still would have never been able to justify punching his lights out, especially in the lobby of the Brooklyn Supreme Court. He did admit that he had been having a problem with that particular ADA for the past month or so. He had heard that the guy wanted to work for the Legal Aid Society as they pay better than the DA's office, but was turned down after the interview.

That was Al's problem to deal with, and he promised me a different ADA would handle the presentation of my case. He pressed a button on his desk console, and when his secretary answered he asked her to locate Julie Finkelstein and ask him to come to his office.

Al and I talked about the old days, and it wasn't long before Finkelstein showed up in Al's outer office. Al introduced us and after briefly filling him in on what had happened, Finkelstein suggested that I send my complainant to lunch and have her back by 1:30 so he could talk to her and have her on the stand by 2:00 p.m. He told me where I could find his office, and asked me to meet him there in about fifteen minutes. He had hoped that by then the Chinese food that he had ordered would have arrived. He suggested that while we ate, I could fill him in on the particulars of the case.

# Chapter 34

**I WAS AGAIN CONTACTED BY THE** Notifications Desk of the Hearing date which had been set for the following Monday. In cases where the defendant is unable to come up with bail money, the defense attorney will usually demand that a Hearing be held within seventy-two hours, which by law the defendant is entitled to. In this particular case the defendant had already been indicted on Felony charges of First Degree Rape and Sodomy, which meant that the impending hearing was primarily to determine the admissibility of the confession. This type of a procedure is commonly referred to as a "Motion to Suppress Hearing".

Since I had the weekend off, I was forced to make the early morning commute by car into downtown Brooklyn. I arrived at the Courthouse at 120 Schermerhorn Street at around 9:15, having first stopped off at the Property Clerks office to pick up the evidence that was collected at the hospital. I signed in at the Police Room just off the cavernous lobby and then went across the street to "Chris's" for breakfast. I sat with a bunch of other cops from different commands, who like me, were regulars. We all spent a lot of time together in Court and had become good friends.

After downing a couple of eggs over light, with hash browns, juice, toast and coffee, I left the restaurant and hurried back across the street to court, not wanting to be late. I took the elevator to the sixth floor and headed for Part 3 B, which is where the Calendar indicated that my Hearing was going to be heard. It was now 9:50 and the Judge was just entering the courtroom. We all stood, as the Bailiff shouted the familiar "Hear yea, hear yea, all rise etc., and sat down as Judge Claude Matthewson ordered everyone to be seated.

Judge Matthewson was a relatively new black jurist, having been appointed to the Bench nine months earlier by the Mayor. He had been a prosecutor with the Brooklyn District Attorney's office for many years and was a highly respected member of the legal community. I had worked closely with him on a number of cases in his former capacity as a prosecutor, and we were on a first name basis up until his time of appointment. After that, I just didn't feel comfortable calling him anything other than "Your Honor", not that I think he would have really cared so long as it wasn't done in public. As he was about to be seated he looked over the Courtroom and for an instant our eyes met, and we exchanged a slight nod of recognition. This was the man who was going to be deciding serious issues concerning this case. It certainly would not benefit the prosecution if even the slightest hint of impropriety appeared to exist between the arresting officer and the Judge, so I had to be careful to remember my place.

It took all of the next half hour for the Judge to wade through old business that had to be taken care of before the cases of the day could be called. There were the Search Warrants that had to be signed for the guys from the Narcotics Division, who patiently waited their turn off to the side of the Bench.

That completed, there were several cases of "Bail Review" that had to be called and disposed of before my case, Docket Number K-27460 was finally called and the defendant was brought into the Courtroom from the holding pens.

The defendant's hands were handcuffed behind his back and the cuffs were not removed until he was seated beside his attorney at the defense table. Mr. Peter Entiocco had been the attorney appointed by the Court to represent him. He was what was referred to as an 18B attorney, which meant that Justin Washington, not being able to afford to pay an attorney was still being represented by one and that the State of New York was footing the bill. Many attorneys, especially those just starting out in private practice signed up for this kind of work and while the fees are much lower that what a well to do client would be expected to pay, it none-the-less was better than sitting in your office waiting for clients to come knocking.

Judge Matthewson asked both the prosecutor and the defense attorney to approach the Bench and a short conference ensued, after which all parties who would be testifying in the case was asked to leave the courtroom. They were to wait outside in the corridor for their turn to testify. In reality, it was a safeguard for the defendant. On the way out of the courtroom I noticed that the rookie, O'Brien was seated in the next to last row, and as I passed him I motioned for him to follow me out the door.

Once out in the corridor, we shook hands. This was the first time that I had seen him in a while, as he was still in his last week at the Academy. We walked over to a relatively quiet corner of the corridor, and I asked him if he had gone over his memo book notes and more specifically what it was that the ADA had asked him to testify about. He looked around nervously and said that he was afraid that I might ask him that question. He went on to say that he had been warned by the ADA that he was not to discuss the case with anyone.

I tried to explain to him that what the ADA had meant was that he shouldn't discuss the case with civilians or the defense attorney. I tried to convince him that he was allowed to discuss it with fellow officers who had participated in the arrest. I went on to say, in a reassuring manner, that all I wanted to do was to make sure that he wouldn't be leaving anything important out of his testimony. I tried to stress the fact that I was not telling him what he should say on the stand, but that this being his first time on the stand was causing me some concern. I reminded him that this was a very serious case and we could not afford to make any mistakes. He told me that he was well aware of the fact that this was a serious case, and that he had no intention of screwing anything up. Those were his exact words and I was tempted to say, "You better not screw it up", but I bit my tongue and I said, "I certainly hope you don't."

Moments later a Court Officer stuck his head out into the hallway and called the victim into testify. A kind of distance had sprung up between the rookie and I and the both of us moved off to stand with other cops.

It wasn't that long before the little girl came out into the corridor looking visibly shaken. It was pretty obvious that she had been crying. As I was about to approach her, O'Brien's name had been called out, again by the Court Officer, and he disappeared into the Courtroom.

The child's mother had begun to tell me how they had asked her daughter to explain what had happened on the roof. Halfway through her testimony, she began to cry and could not resume testifying. I left the mother with her child as she tried to calm the little girl. I didn't like the way things were playing out. My experience had been that both defense and prosecuting attorneys went very gently in the questioning of a young child. If they stepped over the line too far, the Judge would quickly put an end to the questioning. I just couldn't believe that Judge Matthewson would have allowed the defense attorney to intimidate the victim.

O'Brien couldn't have been on the stand more than ten minutes tops, when he exited the courtroom. I could tell by the expression on his face that he had not fared too well on the stand. I caught his eye and he quickly looked away. He then started moving down the hallway toward the bank of elevators.

I started after him, but in the next moment my name was called. I entered the courtroom and walked up to the witness box. I looked over at the defense table and I couldn't help but notice the smirk on the defendant's face. I looked over to the ADA and he didn't look too happy at the moment.

I had a strange feeling that something had gone terribly wrong, even the Judge seemed to be a little uncomfortable in his high backed chair, as he said to the ADA,

"Shall we continue counselor?"

The ADA looked the worst of all. I had spent about an hour with him the previous week going over my testimony in preparation for the hearing and at the time he seemed pretty confident. Now he looked anything but confident and it seemed that the last place on earth that he wanted to be was in this courtroom. It was almost as if, the last thing he was looking forward to was the beginning of my "direct examination".

Based on what I sensed was going on around me, I also was filled with a feeling of impending doom. The prospect of finding out what had gone wrong wasn't particularly appealing to me. From the moment that I had made this arrest, screwing the case up somewhere along the line, was one of my biggest fears, and now it seemed that that fear was about to become a reality.

# Chapter 35

**IT IS AT TIMES LIKE THIS THAT** Peter Entiocco wishes that he had become a doctor instead of a lawyer. As a physician, he was convinced that he would always be helping people. As an attorney, he now found himself defending one of the lowest forms of life on the face of the earth, a "child molester."

After having graduated law school, Peter had signed on with the Legal Aid Society for a couple of years before starting out in his own private practice. He choose being a Legal Aid attorney, not so much for the money which was better than what the DA's people received, because he felt more compelled to defend individuals rather than prosecuting them. He didn't feel that he was naïve when it came down to the guilt or innocence of the people that he represented. Contrary to what his clients would like you to believe, more than ninety percent of them had in fact committed the crime for which they had been arrested. His main concern was more with assuring that they had been afforded all the protection of the law. Namely, that as guaranteed by the Constitution, they were presumed innocent until proven guilty. It was the State's job, with all of its power and resources, to prove beyond a reasonable doubt the guilt of the person charged with the crime. Peter didn't enjoy seeing an obviously guilty individual go free. It upset his sense of fairness, in that if you violated society's rules, you should be held accountable for your transgression. What upset him even more, however, was when the individuals who were given the responsibility of enforcing the law, namely the police, adopted the policy of "the end justifying the means".

In his opinion, that was a very dangerous premise on which to proceed and such a policy had to be guarded against and fought against vigorously, whenever and wherever it was encountered.

Feeling that way as strongly as he did however, didn't make defending this particular client any easier for him especially since he was the father of a ten year old daughter, himself.

He could have just as easily refused to take the case, citing his personal distaste for this type of crime, but that excuse probably wouldn't have sat too well with either the presiding Judge, or with his peers in the Bar Association. Therefore, he had politely thanked the Judge for the referral, and thoroughly researched the material that had been delivered to him by the DA's office

The prosecutor in a criminal case is required by law to provide the defense attorney with all written documents, including taped video confessions and any other material that could be used as evidence against the defendant. Peter therefore had had the pleasure, if you could call it a pleasure, of viewing a copy of the videotaped confession that had been made of his client. A confession in which he candidly describes what he had done to the victim. Without ever even having met his client, he had already developed an intense dislike for the man. Peter's only consolation was the fact that regardless of how hard he might have to fight for this creep, in the end he would be convicted and sent to prison for a very long time. While every lawyer strives to win his case in Court, this was one case, the losing of which would not terribly upset him.

He had visited his client at the House of Detention and had assured him that he would do everything in his power to work out a plea bargain with the DA's office. However exactly what kind of a deal he couldn't even speculate about until he had an opportunity to discuss the case with the prosecutor.

To his surprise, Justin wanted no part of a plea bargain, if it meant going to prison. I had all I could do to keep from laughing in his face. He didn't want to go to prison. I couldn't believe what I was hearing. What the hell did he expect them to do, appoint him Deputy Mayor for Community Affairs? He had raped a little girl and forced her to commit sodomy. He was an animal and he had the nerve to say that he didn't want to go to prison. He's lucky the cops didn't just throw him off the roof that night. Had it been a white girl, they probably would have. It would've been very easy for them to claim that he jumped rather than be arrested, and he never would have survived the fourteen story fall to dispute their claim. Now he had the audacity to think that he was in a position to dictate the terms of a "Plea Bargain". I told him that he should have thought of that before he agreed to make the videotaped confession.

I left the House of Detention disliking him even more than I had before. However, I did make good on my promise to call the DA's office the following day and set up an appointment with the prosecuting ADA to go over the merits of the case.

I arrived at the Municipal Building a little after three that following afternoon, explained to the receptionist who I was and that I was expected. Within a matter of minutes, after having conferred with someone on the telephone, she directed me to the office where the meeting was to take place.

The ADA assigned the case listened while I explained the conditions that my client insisted on in return for a guilty plea. After patiently hearing me out, he informed me that there wasn't going to be any deals made with respect to this particular case. He continued, saying that the District Attorney's office was prepared to prosecute this case all the way to a guilty verdict. He told me to tell my client that he was not going to "walk" on this one as he had on the murder of his daughter.

I said that I was only aware of a prior conviction of Armed Robbery of a liquor store during which he had been shot a couple of times and for which he had done some "hard time" in State prison. I knew nothing about a murdered daughter and the revelation was quite a shock to me.

None–the–less, my counterpart was well aware of the fact that I was duty bound to defend the client to the best of my ability. Although, I think he sensed by the look on my face and my attitude that I really didn't have my heart in what I had been directed by the Court to do, namely provide the "creep" with the best defense possible. We agreed on a Hearing date, and I shook hands with him before leaving his office.

While riding down in the elevator I pondered exactly what the chances were of my client being found "not guilty", and decided that they were less than zero and you know what, I was glad! The streets of New York would be a lot safer without him being on the loose.

The courtroom had been cleared of all potential witnesses, and the ADA was now calling the victim to the stand. She was such a small child, and I remembered my client's confession in which he stated that he had though that she was younger than what she actually was. The ADA took her back to the day that the incident actually occurred, and she stated, in a small child's voice, what had happened to her. She became emotional when she was asked to look around the courtroom and point out to the court the person who had done those things to her. She haltingly pointed to my client who was seated next to me at the defense table, and then she began to cry. The female court officer attempted to comfort her, handing her some tissues and when it seemed that she had regained her composure the Judge looked in my direction, and in a somewhat irritated voice said,

"You may cross-examine the witness."

"I have no questions, Your Honor." I replied while coming to my feet. And with that the Judge excused the witness. My client turned toward me, and in a whispered voice said,

"What gives, man?" I guess the look I gave him conveyed my answer, namely for him to shut the hell up. As he looked away his eyes cast downward in what I would have liked to believe was some sense of remorse, but I sincerely doubted that he was capable of such feelings.

The next person to be called was the partner of the arresting officer. He had escorted the defendant from the scene to the police station. His testimony shed no new light on the case as I had been provided with photocopies of this officer's and the arresting officer's memorandum book entries, which I had read. It was obvious that he was a "rookie", as he was quite nervous on the stand.

When it was my turn to cross-examine the witness, I decided that I might as well at least earn my fee, as well as prevent my client from filing an appeal based on an "inadequate defense", so I simply got to me feet and approached the witness.

"I have only a few questions officer", I began and immediately noticed the witness tensing up a bit.

"Officer O'Brien, you said in your testimony that after the defendant was arrested and handcuffed on the roof, that he was walked down fourteen flights of stairs, and out the back door of the building. Is that correct?"

"Yes, that's correct." He replied.

"You further stated that you and the defendant were transported to PSA 2 in an unmarked patrol car. Is that correct?"

"Yes it is." He replied and began to relax a little, crossing his legs.

"Did you have an occasion to converse with the defendant while on your way to the PSA?"

"Could you repeat that question, I'm not sure that I understand what you are asking"

Either the kid is being "cute" with me or he's just not too bright.

"Sure, I'll repeat the question officer. Did you say anything to the defendant, or did he say anything to you while riding to PSA 2?

"No, I didn't say anything to him, nor did he say anything to me.' He replied.

"When was it then that you advised him of his Rights, as you previously testified that you did?"

"While at the PSA, while we were waiting for Officer Caporusso to arrive. I thought it might be a good idea. So, I advised him of his Rights."

"Hadn't Officer Caporusso already advised him of his Rights while you both awaited the arrival of the unmarked car that eventually took you to the PSA?"

"Yes he did, but I thought it might be a good idea to advise him again."

"And what did the defendant say, might I ask, after you again advised him of his Rights?"

"He refused to make a statement; he didn't want to say anything." said the rookie.

Upon hearing that response I froze in my tracks and looked over at the prosecutor's table. The ADA's face had turned ashen as he looked up at the police officer in disbelief. Without even realizing it this officer had just caused the whole confession to become inadmissible as evidence. I could hardly believe what I'd heard, and the significance of the officer's last statement certainly wasn't lost on the Judge either who was now also staring in disbelief at the officer.

"I have no further questions, Your Honor." I decided at this time to quit while I was ahead, and took my seat at the defense table.

The Judge looked toward the ADA and said,

"Is there to be any re-direct counselor?"

At that point the ADA was already on his feet advancing toward the witness box where the officer sat, somewhat uncomfortably realizing that he had said something that he shouldn't have said.

"Officer O'Brien", the prosecutor began, "When you testified that the defendant refused to make a statement, isn't it true that what you meant to say was that the defendant had remained silent and that at that time he had not made any statements?"

"Objection Your Honor", I quickly interjected while rising from my chair.

"The prosecutor is leading the witness!" I said.

"Objection sustained" said the Judge.

"Officer O'Brien", the prosecutor continued, "Did the defendant, at any time make a statement to you?"

"No he didn't, he refused!" continued the officer, obviously very nervous by now.

"Officer, please just answer the question yes or no?" the ADA stated in a now obviously hostile tone of voice.

Once again I was out of my chair and on my feet.

"Objection, Your Honor, the prosecutor is badgering the witness."

"Objection sustained" again said the Judge, adding.

"I think the officer's testimony is quite clear, the defendant clearly made his intent to not answer any questions quite obvious. I must therefore rule that any statements or confessions made after that point in time are clearly inadmissible as evidence against the defendant, as they could not have been voluntarily made. If you have no further questions of the witness, I will excuse him. I don't think that the defense has any further questions at this time, do you councilor?"

"No, I don't Your Honor" I said.

"You are excused officer. Call your next witness councilor, and we will go on to the other physical evidence."

The ADA was visibly shaken, as the decision of the Judge had severely hurt his case by eliminating the videotaped confession. He still hadn't recovered when the next witness, the arresting officer entered the courtroom.

The irony of the whole situation was that in reality, my client by his own admission to me hadn't really refused to make a statement. He had told me that his intent was not to say anything and therefore he had remained silent. His decision to confess had been brought about by his conversation with the detectives who he claimed had scared the shit out of him. The "rookie" officer, lacking experience, had violated the cardinal rule of testifying and that is to never volunteer information while on the stand. For the most part, you should just answer the questions posed to you with a yes or no response.

Without any conscious effort on my part, I had inadvertently altered the course that this case might have taken and the thought that my client because of this, might go free, frightened me to no end....

# Chapter 36

**THE ADA, UPON THE SUBTLE PRODDING** of the Judge, slowly came to his feet and walked toward the witness box where I sat. I could sense by his demeanor that I was in for one hell of a grilling. My mind raced through the series of events, since my first contact with the defendant, trying to pick out anything unusual that might have occurred. All that came to mind was the short period of time when I had left him in the custody of Joe and Harry. Something had probably happened while I was off getting the coffee and donuts. What exactly, I didn't know. I was sure of the fact that the defendant had not been physically abused, as there were no visible signs of any injuries. If they had intimidated him, as I suspected they had, it was a matter of his word against theirs. It had been the defendant's idea to voluntarily make the videotaped confession; at least, that's what Joe had told me.

Wait a minute I thought to myself, the only witnesses to testify thus far had been the victim and the rookie, O'Brien. The question of what might have happened while the defendant was being questioned by Joe and Harry hadn't even been touched upon yet. The problem had to revolve around O'Brien's testimony. The victim certainly couldn't be faulted for her actions. What the hell could O'Brien have said to create this obvious atmosphere of gloom and despair? I should have grabbed O'Brien before he left the courthouse! Had I done that I wouldn't be in the situation that I now found myself, wondering what the hell he had said during his testimony on the stand.

The ADA began questioning me in a manner that I was quite familiar with, having over the years spent a considerable amount of time testifying in Court.

"Officer, would you please state your name, title, and assignment."

His subsequent questions and my responses brought me quickly to the point when I had returned to the PSA, after having seen to it that the victim and her mother had been taken to the hospital. However, his next question caught me completely off guard.

"Officer, upon your return to the station house and once gain making contact with Officer O'Brien, did there come a time when Officer O'Brien informed you that the defendant refused to make a statement?"

"No, he didn't tell me any such thing" I said, breaking the rule about sticking to yes or no answers only!

"Did you have any conversations at all with Officer O'Brien during that period of time, that is, immediately upon your return to the PSA?"

"Yes, I did."

"Could you be more specific please?" said the ADA

I very slowly began, being very careful of my choice of words, clearly realizing now what the problem was, explained that I had casually asked Officer O'Brien if the defendant had said anything while I was gone, and that his reply had been, "No". It was plain to me that the only thing the defendant had talked about with O'Brien since their arrival at the PSA was his need to use the bathroom. I continued on to explain that after I had permitted the defendant to use the toilet, I again sat him down and very carefully explained to him exactly what his Rights were.

"Was it then that he agreed to make a statement?" asked the ADA.

The defense attorney was out of his chair objecting before I had even had a chance to formulate my answer.

"Objection, Your Honor, the decision to rule the confession inadmissible has already been decided by Your Honor. Does the District Attorney feel that it is in his power to overrule the decision of the Court?"

"Objection sustained, and a point well taken, I might add." said the Judge.

"Mr. District Attorney," the Judge continued,

"I have ruled in the matter of the confession, and it appears that your line of questioning is an attempt to undo that decision. My correctness in ruling as I did may be argued on Appeal, after the trial, should the defendant be found guilty. Can this Officer testify to the collection of the physical evidence at the hospital? If not, I suggest that barring any questions on the part of the defense, I will excuse this witness."

"I have no questions of this Officer." I was quick to announce.

"Then the witness is excused. I would like at this time to take a short recess, during which time I would like to see both councils in my chambers." said the Judge.

The Bailiff quickly came to his feet and shouted, "All rise, this Court will take a short recess."

With that said the Judge rose from his chair and left the courtroom entering a nearby door that led to his chambers. The ADA asked me not to leave but to wait for him, while he finished with the Judge. I told him that I would be out in the corridor.

Lt. Durenno and Sergeant Mulhern were waiting in the corridor for their turn on the stand, so I brought them up to speed on where the case stood. The fact that the Judge had ruled negatively on the confession's admissibility meant that neither of them would be called to testify about the part they had played in the investigation. Joe, being a Detective Lieutenant, after hearing how O'Brien had screwed up on the

144

stand, swore that he would "get" the rookie, come hell or high water. At the same time he began that habit he had of clearing his throat whenever his stress levels got too high. Harry on the other hand felt that we were both overreacting and crying over spilt milk. Harry's solution to the problem was for the three of us to hit a local bar and down a few beers. It made no difference what-so-ever to Harry that it wasn't even 11:00 o'clock yet.

Joe, being Harry's boss, looked angrily over at him. As usual the look was lost on Harry who was already in the process of checking his wallet to see how much money he had squirreled away for his favorite past time.

Harry announced that he would be in the bar around the corner if we needed him for anything. As Harry walked toward the elevators, Joe looked at me and said.

"One of these days I'm gonna give him a complaint for insubordination."

"Sure you are, Joe." I said, and had to laugh as it was Joe's favorite expression. He had come on the job two full years ahead of me. We had worked together at first in uniform, and then for a number of years in plainclothes until he had been promoted to Sergeant. We kept in touch over the years but our careers led us in different directions. He went on to become a Detective Lieutenant, and was assigned to the Major Case Squad. I went into Special Investigations for the Chief of Patrol. In all those years as a boss Joe had never once hurt anyone with a "Complaint" of any sort. He put a lot of criminals behind bars, but him hurting a fellow cop, would never happen, not in this lifetime. Harry had been gone no more than five minutes when the ADA exited the courtroom and came over to where we were standing.

He said that the Judge was concerned as to whether the case could go forward without the confession. He needed to know from me whether I thought that we had enough to proceed. I told him that we certainly would have been in a much stronger position with the confession; however, having made the arrest while the crime was in the process of being committed, as opposed to a "walk in" type of complaint, made for a strong enough case to go to trial. We also had the victim's torn panties and the medical report from the hospital that would certainly be ruled admissible, as it was properly collected evidence. He said that he felt the same way and would so inform the Judge. He didn't think that I would be needed for further testimony, at least not until the actual trial which would probably not take place for another six to eight months; such was the backlog in jury trials.

We shook hands and he promised to keep in touch. Joe and I took the elevator to the lobby, where we ran into the officers who had taken the victim to the hospital. They were scheduled to testify within the next half hour on the part that they played in the case. I filled them in on what had happened thus far. They couldn't hang around to talk, not wanting to upset the Judge by being late for their appearance, so they quickly headed for the elevators. I turned to Joe and said.

"You don't think they'll screw it up too, do you?" to which he answered.

"If they do, I promise you that I'll give them both a complaint." and we both laughed as we walked outside and headed for the Bar on Court Street to join Harry.

# Chapter 37

**THE MONTHS AFTER THE ARREST FLEW** by, one after another. It was two weeks before Easter that following year that I received word from the DA's office concerning the upcoming trial. I was ordered to report to the DA's office on Monday at 10:00 a.m. sharp to begin trial preparation, as the trial was scheduled to begin the following Monday. Jury selection had just concluded and the trial itself was scheduled to begin in Part 19B of the Supreme Court on Adams Street. I was told that the presiding Judge would be the Honorable Max Weissman, a recent appointee of the Governor. He had worked for many years in the Bronx Criminal Court, where the rumor was that he was very soft on crime. As the story goes, he had been mugged just outside the courthouse one night after finishing up Night Court. Four or five young teenagers had confronted him while he was walking to where he had parked his car. They demanded his wallet and one of them brandished a large knife to show that they meant business. Fearing for his life he turned and tried to run, but  was quickly dragged to the ground where they took not only his wallet, but also his wrist watch and a diamond ring that he was wearing.

A passing police car pulled up to the scene moments after the robbery had occurred, and based on the information supplied by the Judge, a description of the muggers was immediately broadcast over the police radio. Within a matter of minutes, four of the five were apprehended and brought back to the scene so the Judge could identify them. Three of the youths had been found to be in possession of the Judge's property and the fourth was found to be carrying a large knife. When the Judge saw the four individuals he refused to identify them as being his attackers, stating that he hadn't been able to get a good look at them while he was being robbed. It was pointed out to him that they had been found to be in possession of his property when they were apprehended, and his reply had been, "Well maybe the muggers had dropped his property and these fellows had the misfortune of finding it."

He was adamant about not wanting to press charges and the youths had to be released right on the spot. The cops involved, were really "pissed off" at him, as it wasn't every day that you got to save some Judge's ass. Some of them had visions of a "gold shield", to say the least. When in reality, all they got for their efforts was a "Thank you, officers", from a visibly shaken but otherwise unhurt Judge. This incident supposedly took place about ten years ago, when the Judge was in his early forties, by no means an old man.

I was a little worried that this was the Judge who was going to be instructing the jury in my case. That thought alone, was going to be enough to make me a nervous wreck throughout the trial.

For reasons, obvious not only to the DA's office, a black female ADA named Christine Biltmore had been selected to represent the People. She was quite attractive, tall and slender, about 5' 10" in her high heels, which drew attention to her very shapely legs. She had a light complexion with finely chiseled facial features that were complimented with lovely brown eyes. On a scale of one to ten, she rated a definite ten, especially in the figure department what with her trim waist and abundant breasts. Although she didn't look a day over twenty-five, I guessed her age to be around thirty-three, or thirty-four, only because she had been practicing law for the past six years. She had also been very active politically in Crown Heights, one of the predominately black neighborhoods in Brooklyn, often appearing on radio talk shows with members of the Democratic Club. It was rumored that she had been married for a short period of time, but was now divorced. It was thought that her former husband had difficulty handling her success, and had turned to booze and other women. In the legal community she had a very good reputation as a prosecuting attorney, and had won her share of "big cases". She had grown up in the City, and was proud of the fact that she was a product of the public school system, having graduated from Girls High School in Brooklyn. After graduating from Brooklyn College with a degree in Political Science, she was accepted to Brooklyn Law School where she graduated fourth in her class. It was thought that someday she would be the first black female elected to the post of District Attorney of Kings County.

After spending an hour with her, going over the details of the case, I was almost tempted to move back into the city so that I too could vote for her if she ever decided to run for political office. Such was the warmth and magnetism that she exuded. She was very optimistic about winning the case, but was also quick to point out that the outcome was going to rest very heavily on the testimony of the victim. She had spent several hours with the victim, going over her testimony and was pretty sure that she would hold up well under cross examination. However, once someone was on the stand it was that person and that person alone, who had to convince the jury that they were being truthful.

Before we parted I made a point of asking her if she had an opportunity to go over the testimony of the rookie, O'Brien and if she was familiar with what he had testified to at the "Motion to Suppress Hearing"?

"That fiasco!" she joked, had been gone over thoroughly by the DA's office. As far as calling the rookie to testify, she wasn't sure if that would be necessary. She intended to call him in for an interview and after hearing what his testimony would be, would then decide on whether or not to put him on the witness list. He couldn't do any damage if he wasn't called to testify. However she couldn't allow what she was doing to become common knowledge. Should the defense attorney become aware of her plan, he could subpoena O'Brien for the defense, assuming that it could help his case. She also reminded me that whatever she decided to do would have to ultimately be approved by her boss.

Before we parted, I casually said that perhaps after all of this was over maybe we could plan to have lunch together. She smiled and while looking at me said,

"Maybe we could make it a victory celebration!" and on that positive note I left. I was already looking forward to the day that the prospective jury would bring in a verdict of "guilty"!

It must have been around noon when I finally exited the Municipal Building on Fulton Street and I had to decide what to do for the rest of the day, According to Departmental Rules and Procedures I was supposed to return to the PSA, change into uniform and take a foot post for the remainder of the day tour. I could instead, bend the rules a bit and pass a few hours in the movie house over on Court Street watching a "skin flick". I thought that I would head back to the PSA around 3:30, arriving too late to be assigned a post. I had promised my daughter that I would be home for her birthday party, so I couldn't afford to get involved with anything that would force me to stay in the city. It had been quite some time since I'd taken in a movie, so I decided to treat myself to seeing one.

I walked the two blocks over to Court Street and feeling a little hungry, decided to have a slice of pizza with something to drink before going in to see the show. The posters on display outside the theater promised a couple of real hot flicks.

Rather than going into the restaurant, what with the day being sunny and all, I decided to order the pizza while standing outside. The large front window of the place, once opened outward, provided a counter at which a person could stand and eat his pizza without having to enter the premises. It also made girl watching, a favorite pastime of mine a lot easier since you could eat your pizza while admiring the attractive females that paraded by.

This particular place also made excellent pizza. I should have been content with ordering just one slice, considering the weight I had put on, but I just couldn't stop myself from having a second slice. It was the second slice that literally saved my ass. The movie house is located right next to the pizza place, and I had just taken a bite out of my second slice, when out of the theater comes marching six angry individuals, four of whom I recognize from around the court house as being cops. Following closely behind them, are what had to be three bosses from Internal Affairs, recognizable by the fact that all three were dressed in suits. Just as this small crowd spilled out onto the sidewalk, with the cops in "civvies" all trying to explain at once what they were doing in the movie house, a light blue twelve passenger van driven by the fourth member of the "IAB" team pulls up to the curb.. The senior IAB guy, probably a Captain, orders everyone into the van and off they go probably to the old eight-four precinct, home of the local Internal Affairs Unit.

"But for the craving of another slice of pizza, there go I", I thought to myself. With half of my second slice still in my hand, I walked over to the cashier's booth and asked the cute looking Hispanic girl who sold tickets, what had happened? Not knowing or perhaps not realizing that I was also a cop, she said that the theater manager had gotten fed up with having to let cops in free when they showed their badges, decided to call headquarters and make a complaint. The guys in the suits had arrested the cops for getting in the theater without paying.

Apparently the six guys who got caught, were like me, finished up in Court, and were trying to kill a few hours before heading back to their Commands. They had probably "tinned" their way into the movie house, so as to avoid paying the $5.00 ticket fee. They were unfortunately in the wrong place at the wrong time! That infraction just might cost them a lot more than the $5.00 admission charge, at the very least a couple of weeks pay. Had they been civilians and not cops, the worst that could have happened to them was maybe a $25.00 fine for "Theft of Services".

Needless to say, I decided to forego, "Sex Starved Wanton Women", and walked back to Court where I had parked my car. It was now a little after 1 p.m., so I decided to take a nice leisurely drive back to the PSA. Who knows, if it took me until 2:30 p.m. to get back, maybe the Desk Sergeant can find something for me to do around the PSA instead of sending me out on patrol.

Twenty five minutes later I was stopped for a red light at the corner of Pitkin and Hopkinson Avenue. I spot a dispute in progress just off the opposite corner of the intersection. Two men and a woman seemed to be engaged in a heated argument. The tall guy being white seemed totally out of place in this predominately black and Hispanic neighborhood, in addition to the fact that he is wearing a large black ten gallon cowboy hat. The other male appears to be a well-dressed Hispanic, and the female, upon closer inspection was also white. She seems to be trying to drag "Tex" away from the argument, but he is not budging. "Tex" apparently tiring from being tugged at by his girlfriend, shoves her and she falls to the ground. This appears to anger the Hispanic male even further whereupon with his right hand he removes an old fashioned straight razor from the breast pocket of his suit jacket, which he deftly flicks open with a quick twist of his wrist. I now realize that this is going to get real ugly if I don't do something, so I immediately turn right onto Hopkinson Avenue. Having gone through a red light rather than waiting for it to turn green, I narrowly miss being hit broadside by a truck that was crossing Pitkin Avenue. I come to a quick stop in the middle of the street, and jump out of my car. The threat of the straight razor has not been lost on "Tex", who simultaneously pulls what looks like a cowboy's six shooter from under his coat. He points the big gun no more than three feet away and squeezes off two rounds into our Hispanic friend's chest. The impact of the bullets knocks him backwards a couple of feet, and causes him to fall to the sidewalk. He winds up sprawled halfway on the sidewalk and halfway in the gutter, bleeding from the two large holes that have materialized in his back. You can't imagine how quickly this happened. "Tex" was now running south on Hopkinson Avenue with the gun still dangling in his hand, as I shouted "Halt, Police!" I began dodging traffic trying to get across the street to where the Hispanic guy is bleeding all over the sidewalk. Almost immediately a large crowd began to form, and I shouted to no one in particular,

"I'm a Police Officer, call an ambulance!" while trying not to lose sight of "Tex", who was at that moment running into an abandoned four family tenement fifty yards down the sidewalk. The white woman was shouting as I took off running down the street after "Tex",

"Please don't shoot my husband."

Running down the street with my gun in my hand, I entered the abandoned tenement that "Tex", only moments before had disappeared into. I could hear the sound of running footsteps coming from several flights above me and realized that he was heading for the roof. These buildings had been condemned and were due to be torn down in the very near future. He had entered a tenement that was connected to about seven others, so that once on the roof, he could cross the other seven roofs and make it almost all the way to the corner of Hopkinson and Sutter Avenues. The thought momentarily crossed my mind that he could, instead be waiting for me to come out onto the roof so that he could do to me what he had just done to our Hispanic friend. I slowed down and cautiously came out onto the roof in a crouched stance, expecting the worst. It was then that I caught sight of him entering the roof landing door of another building two roofs distant from where I stood. I also heard the sound of the sirens of police cars that were responding to the apparent report of "shots fired-man down". The increasing number of sirens meant that a 10-13 (assist patrolman) had also been called in, as there didn't seem to be an end to the number of cars that seemed to arriving from many different directions and were now congregating on the street down below. Knowing that an intensive search for the gunman was about to begin and not wanting to be mistaken for him, I leaned over the roof's parapet with my police shield held high enough so as to be seen. I got the attention of several officers down on the sidewalk who were about to enter the building, and said in a loud voice, while gesturing with my hands, "He's wearing a large black cowboy hat!" Contrary to popular belief, most cops in situations like this are very quick on the uptake, so the guy's description was now going out over the air on hand held portable radios. I then ran toward the roof landing door that I had seen "Tex" disappearing into. As I slowly entered the staircase with my gun in my hand I was startled by the sight of "Tex" no more than five feet from me coming up the stairs in my direction. Realizing that his escape route was now blocked by the cops below, he decided to go back up to the roof and try another building never realizing that I was only seconds behind him.

I ordered him to continue up the stairs and out onto the roof. Once there I told him to keep his hands high above his head, threatening to blow his head off if he didn't do as I said. I ordered him to the ground with his legs spread wide and his hands behind his back. Once I had him in this position, I handcuffed him and quickly patted him down for the gun. Not finding it, I asked him,

"Where's the gun?" To which he replied,

"What gun?"

"The gun you just shot that Spanish guy with." I said

"What are you talking about?" he said to me.

"Listen pal, I just saw you shoot the guy, so cut the bullshit, and give me some answers!" I said.

"I'm just up here looking for some old pipes to take to the junkyard." He said.

Ignoring his response, I conducted a more thorough search of his person for any other weapons that he might have. Not finding anything else, I stood him up in preparation of walking him down to the street. I had to assume that he had probably tossed the gun off the roof into one of the backyards as he was running from one building to the next. Just then two uniformed 73 cops came out onto the roof, and the three of us headed back downstairs with the prisoner.

The victim had already been removed by ambulance to Lawndale Hospital and it was doubtful that he would survive his wounds. Several detectives arrived and I quickly filled them in on what I had stumbled across. One of them had the nerve to suggest that I turn the prisoner over to them and remain behind to help conduct the search for the missing gun. I guess the look I gave him was not what he had expected as he said,

"Why're you lookin' at me like that, you don't think that I'd actually try to steal your collar, do you?"

With a smile on my face I said,

"Now why would I think something like that, pal?", and with that I placed the prisoner in the back seat of my car. One of the uniform guys who had responded to the roof volunteered to sit in the back with the prisoner, while his partner followed us with their sector car to the 73 Precinct.

While driving back to the precinct with the prisoner, I remembered that today was my daughter's birthday, and I probably wouldn't be able to keep my promise of being home for the party. She would probably be fast asleep by the time I finished up with this one.

Once at the 73, I was met downstairs by another detective who said,

"I'll take it from here kid. Why don't you return to the scene and help with the search for the gun."

I was about to tell him what he could do with his suggestion, when a loud voice from behind the Desk hollers,

"Hey shithead" I turn toward the desk to see who hell is calling me a shithead, and it's my buddy, Lt. Berkowitz. He looks at me says,

"No, not you, I'm talking to Detective Shithead! You go look for the gun. This collar belongs to the kid, you got that?"

The detective clearly never expecting the Lieutenant to takes sides with a Housing cop, looks at him and says,

"Whatever you say boss!" and walks out the front door of the precinct.

# Chapter 38

**TOMORROW IS THE BIG DAY**. For me it's the day my trial will finally begin. I figure it will take about a week, and then I'll know whether I'll be a free man, or more likely, a man facing a lot of years behind bars in some god forsaken prison, in a town whose name I probably wouldn't even be able to pronounce. There's an old sayin in the street, "If you can't do the time, don't do the crime", well it's a little too late to be thinkin' about that sayin'.

I have been locked up now goin' on almost seven months. Three times, I been before the Judge to see if he'll reduce my bail, and three times he refused. So here I sits in the House of Detention. Since I was charged with a sex crime against a kid, they gots me in a type of solitary confinement. They say it's for my own protection. I been up here on the ninth floor where they gots the guys charged with murders, they gots the homos, and then they gots me. We aint allowed out of our cells but one hour a day. Thirty minutes in the mornin' and thirty minutes in the afternoon, and that's only if the weather be good. They gots this big area up on the roof of the building and it's screened in, so you can't hardly jump off the roof. They let me up there with the queens, they figure if I can't protect myself from the fags, then I deserve to get jumped. The killers, they be up there by theyselves, nobody be wantin' to mess with them. They done already killed somebody; one more killin' wouldn't bother them in the least. I guess it could be a lot worse in the general population, always worryin about when somebody gonna stick a shiv in your back.

The "hacks" who work up here are kinda different from the ones that works the regular floors. It's not that they treat you special; it's more like they just don't mess with you as much as them others. I guess workin up here is like a "special gig", and you don't be wantin to do anything to mess that up! Yeah, as long as you calls them "Mister" or "Officer", everythin' be everythin'. My cell is six feet wide by eight feet deep, not the kind of place you could get lost in. I'm sure you seen prison movies on TV, so I don't thinks that I gots to describe it for you. I don't got no cell mate, if that's what you wonderin' about. Like I said before, they try to keep us away from everybody as much as possible.

On Sunday, now that's a different story, all of us up here on the ninth floor gets to go to the Chapel for religious service. I aint never seen so many religious peoples, as I seen in jail. A lot of "goodies" gets passed around in the Chapel, plus it do gets you outta your cell for about an hour. Every Sunday afternoon, we gets to see movies in the Chapel, and depending on who the hack on duty be, you could get hold of one of them queens and she'll gladly sit on your lap, while you both pretend to watch the movie. Being one of the few straight guys on the tier, who hasn't been busted for killin' nobody, my services are in great demand, if you know what I mean! That makes me a regular Sunday afternoon movie goer.

The hacks save the last two rows for the inmates from the ninth floor Segregation Unit. The general population is forced to sit in the front rows, which is jest fine with me. I know for a fact that given the chance, there are some dudes sittin up there that would like nothing better than to cut my balls off. Getting convicted and bein' sent upstate to one of them big prisons, just aint an option that I wants to even think about. Your file is supposed to be confidential, jest for that reason but that aint the way it works. Somebody workin in the Warden's Office or the library, always finds out who got sent up for "messin" with a kid, and from that point on, their life aint worth much.

As far as my lawyer's concerned, the guy has only been around to see me once, since the "Hearing". At first I thought that maybe I should fire his ass, and ask Legal Services to get me another one. He doesn't look like he really gives a shit about me. But, as they say, you can't argue with success. When he got that fagot Judge to throw out my confession, I thought I'd died and gone to heaven. He must know what he's doin' and with a little luck, maybe he can swing some kinda deal with the DA. Jest in case he can't do a deal for me, I been doin' some homework on my own.

Over the last couple of months, I been grabbin' up everythin' that I can gets my hands on at chow time. Doin' like that I been able to put on another 30 pounds, and jest the other day I had the prison barber cut my hair different from what it used to be, figuerin' that maybe the little bitch won't be able to recognize me when we get to Court, specially when the DA lawyer asks her to point to me like they did last time. Them DAs like doing that, it gets them jurors all worked up.

I also bitched to the hacks about getting these real bad headaches when I tried to read, so they sent me to the Doc, and he ordered me to get an eye test. Well, I made sure I failed that test, but good. They fitted me up with a pair of glasses and now I really can't see shit when I wears em. They are the ugliest things I have ever seen, but who gives a shit, they makes me look even more different.

Hopefully, what with the weight I gained and the specs, the kid might not be able to pick me out this time around. That jest might get the jury thinkin' that these white cops just grabbed the first "nigger" they could lay their hands on, and locked him up. I been readin' the law books and it says that even if jest one person on the jury don't think that you done it, then I got to be found "not guilty". There just gots to be one "brother" on that jury that gots to think that I was framed. I knows that I'm hopin' for a long shot, but what else do I got to hope for?

One of the queens that I been servicing got one of her friends on the outside to get me some new threads for the trial, and it's just as well, cause with the pounds that I put on my old shit don't fit me no more.

The big day is almost here, I gots to get me outta here one way or another. Sometimes, for no reason at all shit just happens in these jails. I had heard that one day last month on another floor, a fight broke out in the dayroom. When you gots ninety cons locked up in a not so big room, it don't take much for somethin' to happen. Story has it that a white boy dissed one of the brothers. That brother being big and all, couldn't just let it pass, so he grabbed the white boy in a "bear hug" and then climbed up on one of the metal tables, just showin' off some. Then he raises the boy over his head like them wrestlers do on TV, and for the fun of it he throws the dude aginst the wall. Wasn't no more the four or six feet, but I guess he banged his head bad when he hit the ground.

By the time the hacks get in there and calmed everythin' down, the white dude was already dead. Naturally, none of the brothers remembered seeing anythin'. I heard that he was the only white boy there, so you know aint nobody gonna speak up for him. The hacks couldn't charge all 89 cons with murder, so it was just written up as an accident. These be the things that I just don't even wanna think about, when it comes to somebody findin' out that I been charged with doin' a kid!

# Chapter 39

**I HADN'T BEEN IN THE 73 IN YEARS.** Not since they created Central Booking and boy was I glad to see Lt. Berkowitz. Had anyone else been on the Desk, I would have certainly lost that collar. Unbeknownst to me, two First Grade Detectives from Homicide were already on their way to the 73. They were told that a collar had been made for felony assault with a gun, and that the victim was probably not going to make it due to the severity of his wounds. I was in the squad room filling out the arrest forms and getting ready to go down to Central Booking when the Homicide detectives showed up.

The fact that we hadn't yet recovered the gun really didn't make much of a difference, as I was an actual witness to the shooting. Having recovered the gun would have been the icing on the cake, so it wasn't an absolute necessity. Since it was thought that Julio would soon be history, the guys from Homicide were going to interview "Tex", and hopefully get a confession.

While talking to me, "Tex" kept denying any involvement in the shooting, stating that he didn't know what I was talking about. He insisted that he didn't shoot anyone. That was his story and he was sticking to it. Five minutes with the Homicide detectives and "Tex" was now saying that he acted in self-defense.

What they had been able to determine thus far was that "Tex", which was the only name that he was providing us with thus far, had been having an argument with his common law wife, Francis.

According to "Tex", the Spanish dude seemed to appear out of nowhere and butted into the argument, telling "Tex" to leave the woman alone. "Tex" told the Spanish dude to mind his own business, and an argument between the two of them ensued. Francis tried to pull "Tex" away, but he stood his ground. He wasn't going to let no "wetback" butt into his business. At that point "Tex" became even angrier and when Francis grabbed his arm, he shoved her away causing her to fall to the ground. When "Tex" looked up from where Francis had fallen, the wetback now had a straight razor in his hand and was threatening to cut "Tex". Well, "Tex" wasn't having any of that, so he pulled his gun and fired two shots into the Spanish dude, who then fell to the ground and stopped moving.

According to "Tex", "When somebody, anybody for that matter, threatens to cut you, there's only one thing left to do and that's to shoot the son of a bitch and that's exactly what I did."

When it was pointed out to him that the victim might die from his wounds, his response was,

"It serves him right; it'll keep him from threatening other people, that's for sure."

When we pressed him about the gun that we were unable to find, he stated that he had thrown it as far as he could off the roof into the weeds in the back of the building. He said that he was afraid of getting caught with it. He didn't want to give the police an excuse to arrest him for illegally possessing a gun, since he didn't have a license for it. "Hell back in Texas", he continued, "You don't need a license and everybody has a pistol. It's only in the big cities like New York and Chicago, where only the criminals have guns. Law abiding citizens need to get licenses; it just doesn't make any sense!"

The detectives from Homicide drew up a statement of everything he had said, and he signed it without hesitation. The processing of the arrest went a lot faster than usual. It seems like the homicide detectives have quite a bit of pull, and we sailed through Central Booking in no time at all. In fact, most of the paperwork had been completed before we even left the precinct. "Tex" would be pre-arraigned in the morning, and would be held without bail due to the seriousness of the crime, and the possibility of the victim dying.

It was after 9:00 p.m. when the two homicide guys dropped me off where I had left my car, back at the 73. They promised me that they would keep in touch. Seeing how late it was, and knowing that I had already missed my daughter's birthday party, I decided to stop by Lawndale Hospital to see how Julio was doing.

Lawndale hospital wasn't that far from where the shooting took place, and if Julio lived, he would forever have to be thankful for that. After identifying myself to the security guard in the main lobby, I was directed to the sixth floor and I followed the signs that led to the Surgical Intensive Care Unit. Again I had to identify myself before I was allowed to enter the SICU. I asked the nurse in charge about his condition and was told that he was still critical. I was surprised to see a woman sitting in a chair that had apparently been brought in by the staff and placed near his bedside. It had to be his wife. She was a fairly attractive middle aged Hispanic woman of small stature with dark hair going to gray in areas. She immediately rose from the chair as I entered the room and assuming that I was one of the doctors, began asking me questions about Julio's condition. I introduced myself, explaining that I was the policeman who had arrested the man who had shot her husband. To my surprise, the woman put her arms around me and began crying. She said that she couldn't find the words to thank me for saving Julio. After calming her down, I suggested that she sit back down in the chair, and then I finally got a look at Julio. The poor bastard looked really bad. He had tubes in just about every place on his body that they could put them. He was connected to machines and monitors and had a really big tube taped to his mouth that was connected to a machine that was making a rhythmic hissing sound. It looked like it was breathing for him. One of the hospital staff walked in, and I figured him for an intern, but instead he turned out to be a male nurse.

He attached some small plastic bags filled with liquid to one of the already existing IV lines. Seeing the victim in the condition that he was in made me feel a little queasy. Had "Tex" not fled, but stood his ground, he might have taken a few shots at me and like Julio, I could be lying in a bed like this one with all these tubes running in and out of me. Just the thought of that possibility made me feel even worse.

I told Mrs. Santiago that I would be in the corridor, should she need to speak to me, and I quickly left the room. The male nurse, who had been in the room moments earlier, was now seated at the nursing station. I walked over to him, taking several deep breaths on the way trying to clear my head. I showed him my police shield, and asked him what Julio's chances of surviving his injuries were. His said that they had done all they could in the operating room. He was being given all kinds of antibiotics to prevent any infections from setting in, but that was all they could do. If he made it through the next twenty-four hours, then and only then, would they have a better idea of what his chances would be. Right now it didn't look too promising. I thanked him for his help and asked him if there was a number that I could call in the morning to find out how Julio was doing. He said he wasn't allowed to give out the number to the Nursing Station here in the SICU, but that he could make an exception in this case, as it was official business. He wrote a telephone number on a slip of paper and handed it to me. I thanked him again as he handed me the paper and said I would be in touch. I briefly stepped back into Julio's room and told Mrs. Santiago that I had to be going; she stood and again put her arms around me. I said that I was sure that everything would turn out ok. She said that she and the family were praying for her husband.

Riding down in the elevator, I glanced at the slip of paper in my hand before placing it in my pocket and noticed that alongside the number he has written "Ask for Mario" what do you know, I thought to myself, another "Italian!"

When I finally made it home, my wife Lillian, was just getting ready to go to bed, having just finished watching the eleven o'clock news. She said that she hadn't expected me home this early; otherwise she would've had a dish of macaroni ready. Did I want her to turn on the oven, or would I take care of it myself?

I told her that I wasn't hungry, not to bother. Truth was, I really was hungry, having had nothing to eat but the two slices of pizza at noon, but I was still a little queasy from my visit to the hospital and I wasn't sure if I could keep anything down. I decided to take a shower hoping that the hot water would make me feel better and in the process clear both my head and the hospital odor from my nostrils. By the time I got out of the shower and into bed, Lillian was fast asleep.

I guess I was overtired by that time as sleep didn't come easily and I tossed and turned for quite a while. Knowing that I would have to get up in a few hours made falling asleep even more difficult. The next thing I knew it was 11 a.m... I couldn't believe that I had slept for so long. I couldn't remember ever sleeping for eleven hours straight. I was glad that I had the weekend off and wasn't due back in the city until Monday morning which was when the trial was due to begin. Thinking about work again brought Julio Santiago's name to mind. I decided to call the hospital to see if he'd made it through the night. I went downstairs to the kitchen where Lillian was on her third cup of coffee. I sleepily greeted her with, "Good morning, I have to make a call."

"Who's so important that you have to call on your day off?" she asked.

"I met this nurse at the hospital last night who broke some rules and gave me the direct telephone number to the nurses' station so I could call and find out if the victim made it through the night." I said.

"What victim? You didn't tell me about anyone going to the hospital. What happened?"

"I really didn't feel like talking about it last night. I'll fill you in after I make the call." I said.

"I guess the nurse wasn't that cute. Knowing you, it would have been a lot later than eleven, before you would have rolled in" she said.

"As a matter of fact", I replied. "He was sort of short, bald and a little on the fat side, if you really need to know", I said while waiting for the telephone to be answered.

"Sounds like just your type, Hon! Now I know why you didn't bother me last night after you got out of the shower." she said, not to be outdone.

A female answered the phone and after I told her who I was she said that Mario had gone off duty several hours ago. Yes, Mr. Santiago was doing much better. He had regained consciousness and was being weaned off the respirator.

"No I don't know what that means, but it sounds positive." I said.

There really wasn't much else that she could tell me, so we said our goodbyes, and I hung up the phone. I thought about driving back into Brooklyn and visiting with Julio, but I knew that my wife wouldn't be too happy if I left the house on my day off. I sat back down at the kitchen table and "Lil" poured me a cup of coffee.

"So tell me all about your new love affair. Does he at least have a nice personality?" she said laughing.

Not finding the conversation any longer amusing, I changed the subject, asking if we were still on for dinner with Frankie and Beverly on their boat, which I had been looking forward to for the past two weeks.

"Yes", she replied. "In fact Bev had called last evening to make sure that we hadn't forgotten."

I was looking forward to being with my friend, Frankie and his wife Beverly. He had this beautiful 48 foot Tollycraft. It was still too early in the season to go for a ride, so we would have to satisfy ourselves with a small get together on board while it was docked on the canal in his back yard. It still beat lying in some hospital bed with two bullet holes in your chest and tubes running in and out of your body.

# Chapter 40

"**HEAR YEA, HEAR YEA, ALL RISE**", said the bailiff. "Part 19B of the Supreme Court of the State of New York, County of Kings, is now in session. The Honorable Max Weisman presiding. All those having business in the Court shall be heard. Please be seated."

The first order of business was for the Judge to direct the Court Officers to bring the defendant from the holding cell into the courtroom, to be seated alongside his attorney. This was all accomplished before the jurors were allowed to enter the courtroom. God forbid that the jurors should see the defendant in handcuffs. The rationale being that seeing him in handcuffs might force them to conclude that perhaps he was dangerous. Give me a break, the guys on trial for rape, why wouldn't the jurors think he was dangerous, cuffs or no cuffs.

As the defendant entered the courtroom, I had to take a second look in order to convince myself that it was really him, and that the court officers hadn't brought in the wrong prisoner. So much of his appearance had changed since the last time I'd seen him at the prior Hearing. His hair was styled differently, and having gained a considerable amount of weight, his face was fuller and he appeared shorter than the tall lanky guy that I had encountered on that roof. The eye glasses were the real clincher; they gave him a rather meek and studious appearance that went quite well with the new brown suit that he was wearing. I was sure that the suit hadn't been bought with funds from the Legal Aid Society; someone had apparently gotten hold of his current suit measurements and went shopping for him.

I looked over at the ADA and tried to get her attention, but she was engaged in a quiet conversation with one of her assistants. Azurenthia Williams, the victim in the case was also seated behind the prosecutor's table. While I'm positive that she had seen the defendant being led to the defense table, she didn't so much as even flinch as they made eye contact; in fact it looked like she may have even smiled. This was quite unnerving, as this was the guy who had terrorized and raped her. Had they gotten to her, and was she now on their side? The thought of her not recognizing him was entirely possible. I spent a lot of time with him after the arrest, and I was having some trouble recognizing him.

The jurors were led into the courtroom through a door that was directly to the right of the Judge's bench, and took their seats in the jury box. The twelve jurors, from where they sat, had an unobstructed view of the defendant, as well as the complainant, in addition to the witness stand.

The Judge addressed both the defense attorney and the prosecutor and said,

"Before we begin, are there any last minute requests on either side?"

The defense attorney rose from his seat and said,

"Your Honor, I request that all potential witnesses be asked to leave the courtroom at this time."

"So ordered." said the Judge.

"Bailiff, see to it that the witnesses are escorted from the courtroom now."

As a result of the Judge's order I found myself in the corridor outside the courtroom. I was joined by the two officers who had transported the victim and her mother to the hospital. I also noticed O'Brien standing off by himself, engrossed in reading what appeared to be a paperback novel. Feeling in a somewhat charitable mood I called over to him, inviting him to join our little group. I was also looking for an excuse to talk to him before he took the stand. I wanted to make sure that he had his story straight and that he wouldn't screw up his testimony.

After several minutes of pleasantries and questions about how he liked working in the Bronx, I broached the subject of his upcoming testimony.

"Have you had a chance to sit down with Miss Biltmore, the ADA, and go over your testimony?" I asked.

"Don't worry about me Cappy", he replied. "I'm really sorry about the last time, and you can rest assured that it won't happen again."

"Don't sweat it Bill," I said to him. "That's water under the bridge; just chalk it up to experience."

He took the words right out of my mouth when he next said,

"Did you see how different the perp looks? I almost didn't recognize the guy!"

In a chiding manner I said, "I hope you won't have any problems today, if you're asked to point him out in the courtroom?"

"No, I'm sure I won't have any problems." He said.

The conversation went on to another topic, and I finished recounting the details of the shooting arrest that I had recently made, when the complainant, Azurenthia and her mother exited the courtroom. Her mother didn't look too happy so I went over to find out what was wrong. I asked the mother how Azurenthia's testimony had gone.

"Her testimony went off without a hitch, just like she and the ADA had talked about it. She said how she had met the man outside in front of the building. How he had asked her to help him find a lady that was supposed to live in the building. That he had showed her a medicine bottle, telling her that he had to deliver it to the lady who was sick. How he said that he thought the lady lived on the top floor and could she help him find the lady. When they got off the elevator instead of looking for the lady he made her go to the roof.

"Did she say what happened when they got to the roof?" I asked.

"Yes, she explained all those awful things that he did to her." She said.

"Why am I seeing such sad faces, it sounds like she did well on the stand?" I asked.

"The reason we is so upset is because when it came time to point to the person who attacked her. She turned to the Judge and said that she didn't see him in the courtroom. That's why I'm so upset. That bastard was sitting right there in front of her smilin' all the time with those stupid glasses." At that point the little girl looks up at me and says,

"I'm sorry, Officer Cappy, when they asked me to point him out, I just didn't know who to pick. Nobody looked like the guy who had hurt me back then."

"Holy shit", I said to no one in particular. Just then my name was being called by the Court Officer, who had stepped from the courtroom into the corridor.

I was directed to the witness box and I stood waiting to take the oath. Moments later, after placing my left hand on the bible, I raised my right hand. The Bailiff then said,

"Do you promise to tell the truth, the whole truth, and nothing but the truth?" To which I replied, "I do"

During my swearing in all I could think about was how was I going to fix the fact that the victim couldn't identify the accused.

Myrtle Biltmore the ADA impeccably dressed in a dark business suit approached the witness box where I was seated and began her questioning by asking the standard questions, my name, my rank and where I was employed. Once this was out of the way she moved on to what had been my assignment on the night of October 3rd of last year and more specifically, what had occurred that led me to the roof of 422 Blake Avenue?

I recounted how my partner and I had been on the higher roof of a nearby building, and that I had observed some movement on the roof of 422 Blake Avenue. That, being unable to discern what was occurring I decided to conduct a further investigation and proceeded on foot to the aforementioned address. That upon our arrival we went to the roof of the fourteen story building, and once there, I delayed going out onto to the roof until we could determine exactly what was occurring."

"Officer Caporusso", she began. "Just before you went out onto the roof and placed Mr. Washington under arrest, what if anything did you see him doing?"

I paused before answering. They teach you to do that in the academy.

"From my place of concealment" I stated. "In the darkened stairwell with the door leading to the roof slightly ajar, I was able to see the defendant's upper torso as he appeared to be raising and lowering himself in a distant corner of the roof."

"Was there enough light on the roof," she continued to ask, "for you to be able to see if there was anyone else on the roof?"

"No, there wasn't."

"And could you elaborate more specifically about what you were able to see, with respect to the defendant's actions?"

"I was only able to make out his up and down movements only because his head and upper torso would rise above the top of the roof's parapet, and in so doing, was silhouetted against the night sky."

"For how long of a period of time did you have the defendant under observation, before you decided to go out onto the roof and arrest him?" she asked.

"At the most, one to two minutes." I replied.

"Why did you wait so long before taking action?"

"At the time I wasn't sure of what we had. By that I mean that I wasn't sure of exactly what he was doing and I didn't know if there was anyone else on the roof other than the defendant. I paused to see if anything else was going to happen." I said.

"What prompted you to finally make the decision to go out onto the roof? Had anything happened that caused you to take the action that you did?"

"The defendant" I began, "had apparently heard a noise that...."

"I object Your Honor," said the defense attorney. "The witness is expressing an opinion as to what someone else was thinking."

"Objection sustained, please rephrase your question." said the Judge.

Officer Caporusso, please tell the Court what happened that caused you to go out onto the roof and arrest the defendant."

"From where I was positioned, I could see that he once again stood up, causing him to again be silhouetted against the night sky. I then heard the sound of my partner's police radio quite loudly calling another police unit. It was at that point that the defendant, instead of lowering himself as he had been doing, abruptly turned in my general direction. After hesitating for only a moment he started walking quickly toward the door behind which I was crouched. Not wanting to confront him in the darkened stairwell, which he was only moments from reaching, I stepped out onto the roof and shouted "Police freeze, don't move."

"Did he comply with your order not to move?" asked the ADA.

"No he didn't, at least not initially. However, once I leveled my service revolver directly at the center of his chest from about four feet away, he froze in his tracts, and simultaneously raised his hands above his head." I said.

"I then ordered him to lie face down on the ground, and to place his hands behind his back."

"Did he comply this time?"

"Not immediately." I said. "I had to cock my revolver and place it near his head to make him understand that I meant business."

"Did he say anything at that point?"

"Yes he did." I said

"And what were his exact words."

"He said, "please, please, don't shoot me!" I said

I looked over at the defendant at that moment, and he was shaking his head, as if to say that I was lying.

171

"What happened next, Officer?"

"I handcuffed his hands behind his back." I said

"And where was your partner while all this was going on?"

"He had moments earlier, joined me on the roof."

"When did you first become aware of the fact that there was someone else on the roof in addition to yourself, your partner and the defendant?"

"I had just finished securing the second cuff to the defendant's wrist when I said to the defendant, in an attempt to distract him from my applying the handcuffs. What's going on up here? It was at preciously that moment that I saw the figure of another individual dart out from the same corner of the roof where I had originally seen the defendant coming from. Fearing that it might be an armed accomplice I again shouted, "Police, don't move!, and approached the individual who had stopped running at that point, only to discover that it was a small female child."

"What, if anything, did the child say to you?" she asked.

"She didn't say anything, at least nothing that I could make out. She was crying more than anything else."      "

Could you describe her clothing, more precisely, the condition of the clothing she was wearing?"

"She had on a cloth jacket that appeared to have been pulled off her shoulders, and halfway down her back.

"Objection Your Honor, the witness is making an assumption as to how the complainant's jacket came to be in a certain position."

"Overruled, I think that the Officer, as a trained observer", said the Judge, "is merely describing how the jacket appeared to him upon his visual inspection. Officer, you may continue with your testimony."

"Her blouse" I continued, "was unbuttoned halfway down the front and was outside her jeans, which were pulled up, but neither zippered nor closed at the top."

"What did you then do?"

"I walked the child a short distance away from the prisoner after instructing my partner to cover him. I then asked her what had happened and she stated that the

172

defendant had hurt her, and again began crying. I calmed her down as best I could, and asked her to start from the beginning. She said that she ....."

"Objection, Your Honor, the Officer's testimony constitutes Hearsay, the complainant has already testified as to what she alleges occurred. I see no reason to subject the jury to information that has already been gone over already."

"Objection sustained, the District Attorney will move on to testimony relevant to what the Officer did, and not what the complainant said."

"Officer Caporusso, did there come a time when you had another opportunity to speak with the defendant"

"Yes, there did." I said, looking directly at the Washington who was avoiding my stare by appearing to be more interested in the black female court officer than in what I had to say.

"Could you please tell the Court the substance of that conversation?"

"Upon returning to where my partner had been guarding the prisoner. The both of us pulled him to his feet, at which time he asked me, "Why are you arresting me? I was only trying to help her find the guys that beat her up.""

"On the roof of a fourteen story building?" I asked

"That's where she said that she thought they had run off to hide." He said.

"Objection, Your Honor. The statement was made prior to my client being advised of his Miranda Warnings."

"Objection, overruled" said the Judge, who continued, "The statement, in so far as I can see, was made spontaneously by the defendant without any prompting by the Officer at the time of the arrest. It was an unsolicited statement. I will however order it stricken from the record and will instruct the jury to disregard the defendant's response to the Officer's question concerning a fourteen story building. It appears that it was an attempt by the Officer, however innocent to obtain information from the defendant prior to his "Miranda Warnings.""

"One last question Officer," asked the ADA. "Could you determine from observing the complainant, if she had sustained any injuries?"

"Objection, Your Honor. The prosecutor is asking for a conclusion on the part of the Officer, who is neither a doctor nor a medically trained individual."

"Overruled" said the Judge. "The ADA is asking the Officer once again, as a trained observer what he observed with respect to plainly visible injuries, continue Officer."

"The victim" I said "had a swollen upper lip which blood had been slowly trickling from."

"No further questions, Your Honor." said the ADA.

"Your witness, Mr. Entiocco", said the Judge.

"I have no questions of this witness, Your Honor. But I reserve the right to call the witness at a later time, if necessary." said the defense attorney.

"Officer, you're excused, but please do not leave the courthouse, as you may still be called to testify at a later time." said the Judge.

"At this time" continued the Judge, "the Court will take a short recess, and will both attorneys please join me in my chambers."

"All rise" bellowed the Bailiff, "This Court will adjourn for a short recess, all spectators are asked to please step outside the courtroom"

I slowly walked out of the Courtroom trying to size up the jury's mood as they were being escorted to the jury room. I had no way of knowing if I had undone the damage that had been done by the complainant's inability to point out the defendant in open Court. Only time would tell.

# Chapter 41

**TO SAY THAT JUDGE MAX WEISMAN** was a little concerned about the direction the case was headed had to be the understatement of the year.

When both attorneys were seated in his Chambers, he began the conference by asking the ADA, "Just where the hell is this case going, councilor? The defendant obviously belongs behind bars where he won't be able to prey on little girls. However, if you don't get your act together that's not going to happen. I'm not sure at this point that he would even be convicted of simple assault. I'm worried that this case might already be beyond salvageable. I realize, let me finish!" he went on as the ADA attempted to interrupt him in mid-sentence. "Again, I realize that you could not have in a million years been able to foresee the complainant not being able to identify the defendant, but somebody in your office clearly should have done their homework a little better and prevented the original videotaped confession from being ruled inadmissible."

"Your Honor", began Miss Biltmore "the issue of the admissibility of the confession was determined long before I was even assigned the case. As far as the identification in Court is concerned, neither I nor anyone else could have guessed that the defendant would have been able to so significantly alter his appearance so as to create such a problem."

"Well, where do we go from here?" said the Judge. "If she can't identify him, we literally have no case. We aren't discounting what happened to the poor child. Unfortunately, without the identification, the jury could well believe that someone other than the defendant is the guilty party."

"Begging Your Honor's pardon" said Myrtle. "We must not forget that this is a Jury Trial. If with other testimony, such as the police officer's account, and the physical evidence from the hospital confirming the rape, I feel that I will be able to convince the jury of the defendant's guilt. The victim was hysterical at the scene, so it would be understandable considering the terrifying nature of the crime, for her to be unable to identify her attacker almost eight months later."

"Mr. Entiocco, you have remained silent throughout this discussion. What are your feelings in the matter?"

"As much as I hate to admit it, I'm inclined to agree with Your Honor, even as I find the thought of my client going free, disgusting to say the least. But let's look at the facts of the case. What we have thus far is a victim, who, for whatever reason can't ID her attacker. No defense attorney, and certainly not I, would ever challenge her version of what happened. But, if she is unable to say with certainty that the defendant, Mr. Washington, is the individual who did it to her, I'm convinced that Miss Biltmore has a snowball's chance in hell of winning this one. You both know, as well as I do, that many people, especially those living in the inner cities, believe that the police often lie in order to get convictions. This is true especially where it concerns black defendants and white cops. Again, as much as I hate to admit it, unless the DA's office can come up with one hell of a closing argument, my client in all likelihood will walk out of the courtroom a free man. If that doesn't happen, he'll have one hell of an Appeal."

Court resumed shortly thereafter, and Police Officer O'Brien was called to the stand by the ADA.

"Officer O'Brien, I direct your attention to the night of October 3rd of last year at approximately 6:30 p.m. Did you, on that date and at that time, assist with the arrest of an individual on the roof of 422 Blake Ave, Brooklyn, New York?"

"Yes I did", answered O'Brien.

"Do you see seated in this Courtroom the person that you assisted in arresting that night and if so, would you kindly point him out to the Court?"

"He is the gentleman sitting at the defense table." said O'Brien, pointing in the direction of the defendant.

"Officer, there are two gentlemen sitting at the defense table, could you be more specific?"

"Yes, of course. He's the black individual seated at the table."

"Let the record indicate that Officer O'Brien has identified, Mr. Washington, the defendant", said the ADA

"So noted", said the Judge.

"Officer, when was the first time that you saw the defendant, other than from a great distance to make you so positive of your identification today?"

"I stood less than two feet from him on the roof of 422 Blake Avenue on the night of the arrest."

"Was Officer Caporusso with you when you first made contact with the defendant?"

"No, I was standing inside the building on the opposite roof landing and only came out on to the roof when I heard Officer Caporusso shouting, Halt Police, or words to that affect." said O'Brien.

"And when you came out on the roof, where was Officer Caporusso in relationship to the defendant?"

"He was handcuffing the defendant who was lying face down on the ground."

"To the best of your knowledge was there anyone else on the roof other than you, the defendant and Officer Caporusso?" asked the ADA while looking directly at the Jury.

"Yes", said O'Brien. "There was a little girl who appeared to have been assaulted."

"What happened next?" asked, the ADA.

"I guarded the prisoner, while Officer Caporusso walked the little girl a short distance away, and talked to her." said O'Brien.

"Did the defendant say anything while you were guarding him?"

"Yes, he repeated several times, "I don't know why you are arresting me. I was only trying to help the kid or words to that affect."

"Did you say anything to him?"

"I just warned him not to move, as he kept squirming, trying to turn his body, so that he would be able to see Officer Caporusso and the little girl."

"No further questions, Your Honor." said the ADA

"Mr. Entiocco, do you have any questions of this witness?" asked the Judge.

"Yes, I do, Your Honor" said the defense attorney rising from his chair with a yellow legal pad in his hand.

"Officer O'Brien, how long have you been a police officer?" asked the defense attorney.

"A little over a year." said, O'Brien.

"So then at the time of this arrest you were still a Probationary Patrolman, isn't that correct?" said the defense attorney sarcastically.

O'Brien stiffened ever so slightly in his chair at the attorney's change in tone.

"Yes it is, I was performing field training  on a four to twelve tour with Officer Caporusso."

"Quite an exciting night, wouldn't you say?"

"Objection, Your Honor, the question is both immaterial and irrelevant."

"Objection sustained." said the Judge.

"Officer, I really don't have too many more questions for you, so please bear with me a bit longer. On the night in question, your prior testimony at the Preliminary Hearing was that you were secreted, I think that was the term you used, inside the building on the roof landing. Doing what might I ask? Were you observing anything or were you just taking it easy?"

O'Brien, feeling more at ease with the defense attorney's manner, had begun to relax a bit. However, with that last comment, he was again unnerved and scowled at the attorney.

"I was doing what I had been told to do, namely to watch the door. In the event that, whoever was on the roof tried to escape through that door, my job was to stop him. That's what I was doing, Councilor."

The defense attorney's tactic, thought the DA, was to antagonize the Officer a bit and it had worked.

"Did you know for a fact that someone was actually on the roof when you arrived?"

"Yes I did, both Officer Caporusso and myself had seen someone on the roof while conducting a check of the roof of a nearby building."

"And how far was it from where you were to the other building located at, 422 Blake Avenue?" asked the defense attorney.

"A couple of blocks, at the most" said O'Brien.

"And how long did it take you and Officer Caporusso to walk those couple of blocks, or did you drive the distance in a car?"

"No, we walked at a fairly brisk pace; it took about three or four minutes."

"So what you are telling the Court is that while you waited on the roof landing of 422 Blake Avenue, you were no longer absolutely certain as to whether or not the individual you had seen four minutes earlier, was in fact, still where you had last seen him. Isn't that correct?"

"Well, I thought that he might still be there" said O'Brien.

"Officer O'Brien, when you finally did exit out onto the roof to join your fellow Officer and when you approached the defendant who was lying face down on the ground being handcuffed, is it not true that Officer Caporusso had his gun out and had it up against the defendant's head?"

"No, it isn't true, Officer Caporusso had his gun in his holster" said O'Brien, now visibly upset at the direction of the defense attorney's questioning.

"So, what you are saying" said the defense attorney,

"Is that at no time while on the roof of 422 Blake Avenue did you see Officer Caporusso point his gun at the defendant, is that correct?"

"Yes, it is" said O'Brien.

"I have no further questions, Your Honor."

"Does the District Attorney have any further questions of this witness?" asked the Judge.

"No further questions, Your Honor."

At that point, Myrtle was hoping that the jury hadn't picked up the inconsistency between the two officers testimonies. That Caporusso's gun was out of his holster and pointed at the defendant's head when O'Brien came out onto the roof, and not as O'Brien had testified.

For whatever reason, Officer O'Brien had lied about how the collar had gone down. He probably thought that he needed to protect his partner from being accused of the use of excessive force. When what he actually did was drive another nail into the coffin that this case was quickly becoming. She had no intention of drawing any attention to this detail. These were the types of details that the defense would hang on to, that could create the reasonable doubt of the defendant's guilt.

The next witness was Police Officer Roberts, the officer who had transported the victim and her mother to the hospital. He had assumed custody of the evidence collected at the hospital, namely the victim's panties and the glass slides showing the semen that had been recovered from the victim's vaginal area. All of this evidence, plus the ER doctor's report which both sides had stipulated to, was accepted into evidence and appropriately marked as People's exhibits 1, 2 and 3, respectively.

The ADA came out into the hallway, where we were still gathered, and said that the Court was recessing for lunch, and that we were to be back, no later than 2:00 p.m., which would be when she would begin her "Closing". Seeing that somewhat anxious look on her face, I thought better than to ask her if she wanted to join me for lunch. She said something to the effect of having to re-write parts of her "Closing", and that we should make sure that we were not late in getting back to Court.

# Chapter 42

IT WAS AFTER 2:30 P.M., when we were allowed back in the Courtroom. The Judge came out, and we went through the process of standing while he took his seat, and then sitting back down again. The defendant was led back into the Court, escorted by the two Court Officers. Moments later the jury was escorted back in and took their seats in the Jury Box.

"Miss Biltmore, you may begin your closing argument" said the Judge.

"Thank you Your Honor" said the ADA, as she approached the Jury.

"Ladies and gentlemen of the Jury, the time has finally arrived when each and every one of you needs to fulfill your responsibilities as jurors in what we familiarly call the Criminal Justice System."

She continued, "Each and every one of you has been carefully chosen from dozens of prospective jurors. You twelve have been chosen because you have demonstrated by your answers to many questions that you are unbiased and that you will honestly weigh all the evidence that has been presented.

Based on that evidence and that evidence alone, you will arrive at an honest and just verdict. You have heard a lot of testimony, some of which unfortunately may have seemed contradictory. However, I am sure that if you look at all the evidence, rather than dwelling on a few inconsistencies, you will come to the conclusion that the complainant was raped and forced to commit an act of sodomy and that she did it out of fear for her life. You will also arrive at the incontrovertible conclusion that the defendant, Justin Washington, and no one else committed those heinous crimes against a defenseless child. I thank you."

"Mr. Entiocco, if you please" said the Judge.

"Ladies and gentlemen of the jury" began the defense attorney, as he slowly walked to a point just in front of the Judge's bench, where he remained, not quite facing the jury.

"To my left" he began, "sits the victim of a terrible, terrible crime. I'm sure I speak for all of us when I say that no one should ever have to endure what this poor child has gone through. She will be emotionally scarred for the rest of her life."

"To my right" and he gestured to his client seated at the defense table, "Sits the individual who has been accused of committing these heinous crimes. Here to decide his guilt or innocence sits you, the jurors."

He gestured towards the jurors with his hand and continued on in a soothing voice.

"You, the jurors are in between, and rightly so because it is up to you from this point forward to examine the evidence that has been presented and to determine whether or not Mr. Washington is indeed guilty or not guilty of the crime perpetrated against this child, or is he also a victim of the system, himself? A victim of events to which he has become an unwilling participant The victim by her own account is unable to point to Mr. Washington and say, "He did it to me" even though it was alleged that they spoke to each other, first in the street and then again while they rode up fourteen floors in an elevator. "A minor inconsistency", that is what the Prosecutor would have you believe, I think not! The two police Officers that arrested Mr. Washington both testified at length, about what happened on the roof on the fateful October evening.

Both Officers are trained observers, and yet they contradict each other with respect to who had whose gun out and pointed at Mr. Washington. Yet another minor inconsistency! How many more minor inconsistencies are we to allow before we become convinced of the fact that maybe a tragic mistake, on the part of the two conscientious, albeit perhaps overzealous, Police Officers, has occurred?"

"The judge will shortly be giving you your instructions regarding the law in this case, but before he does that, I would like to remind you of one of the basic tenants of our system of justice and that is that an individual is presumed innocent until proven guilty. It is up to you, the jurors to decide the innocence or guilt of Mr. Washington. I would like to add that if reasonable doubt exists in the mind of even one of you, then you must find the defendant Not Guilty of all the charges."

"We have had one tragedy in the person of the victim; let us not compound that tragedy, with yet another one, in the person of Mr. Washington, who stands before you innocent. Thank you."

After the Judge had instructed the jury on the law in the case, they were escorted out of the Courtroom and into the jury room to deliberate.

Everyone was asked to vacate the Courtroom, and as it was still early, some of us went across the street to the "Chock Full O'Nuts shop for coffee.

I had mixed feelings about how the case would go. I knew we had made some blunders, but I none-the-less believed that justice would prevail, and scum like Washington would not go free. I wandered back into the building a little after five, just as it was announced by one of the Court Officers that the jury would be returning with a verdict.

Everyone concerned with the case, save the defendant, who was being held in a nearby cell, sat in the courtroom and anxiously waited for the jury to be led in.

We knew the time was near, as the defendant was once again brought into the courtroom

We all stood as the Judge entered and took his seat behind the bench. The jurors were led in and took their seats in the Jury Box. The Judge then asked the Jury foreman to stand.

He asked the foreman if the jury had reached a verdict. The foreman replied that yes they had. He then again asked the Bailiff to retrieve the slip of paper from the foreman on which the verdict was written. The Judge, after looking at the verdict handed it back to the Bailiff who then returned it to the foreman.

The Judge then, in a clear and loud voice said,

"Will the defendant please rise and face the Jury."

Washington nervously got to his feet. The fact that the Jury had been out so short a time, usually signaled a guilty verdict and that was what was scaring him the most.

"Mr. Foreman of the Jury", said the Judge. "With respect to the count of Rape in the First Degree, how do you find the defendant, guilty or not guilty?"

"We the jury find the defendant, Not Guilty, Your Honor" and with that a loud groan came over the courtroom, to which the Judge banged his gavel and exclaimed, "Order in the Court"

"To the charge of Sodomy in the First Degree, how do you find the defendant, guilty or not guilty?"

"We, the jury find the defendant, Not Guilty, Your Honor" repeated the jury foreman.

"The defendant having been found Not Guilty of all charges is hereby released from the custody of the Department of Corrections, and is ordered released. Case Dismissed"

# THE END

.

# EPILOGUE

One month later, on May 15, three armed men entered a supermarket in Jackson Heights, Queens, and announced a stick-up!

Acting on an anonymous tip, three plainclothes officers, armed with shotguns, had been hiding in one of the rear stock rooms.

An ensuing gun battle between the police and the stick-up men left two of the robbers severely wounded and the third dead!

A search of the dead man's pocket disclosed the business card of an attorney. The name on the card was Mr. Peter Entiocco, Esquire.

The wallet of the deceased gunman was recovered from his back pocket. A recently issued driver's license was recovered bearing the name Justin Washington.

www.ingramcontent.com/pod-product-compliance
Lightning Source LLC
Chambersburg PA
CBHW051910170526
45168CB00001B/318